D0122215

Praise for *Keeping the Millennials*

"'The Millennials are coming! The Millennials are coming!' In this important and timely work, you have the tips and tools that will assist you to more effectively acknowledge and appreciate the values, mores, and culture of this growing element of our workforce. Based on the authors' solid research, you will learn tested techniques to better understand Millennials and to create a more harmonious work environment. Take their advice and 'just do it.'"

—Edward E. Scannell,
CMP, CSP Past National President, ASTD, MPI, and NSA
Coauthor of McGraw-Hill's *Games Trainers Play* series

"The most successful organizations are those that achieve 'best in class' financial results while growing a vibrant culture built on trust and respect for individuals. Joanne and Jan have identified the priorities of the Millennials and have given us expert tools, advice, and ideas to enable our organizations to be winners."

—Bill Mills
Vice President of Human Resources,
GSK Consumer Healthcare North America

"In my 34 years with the University I can certainly be a testament to the Millennials being unique. This is a must-read not only for corporate leaders but also coaches and educators. It's filled with practical tips based on solid research."

—Carol Sprague
Senior Associate Athletic Director
University of Pittsburgh

"Any CEO who is searching for a competitive edge will find *Keeping the Millennials* to be THE BEST BOOK YET for attracting and retaining the most talented and brightest employees."

—Mary Del Brady
President and CEO
RedPath Integrated Pathology, Inc.

"Joanne and Jan hit the nail on the head! Not just the large companies but small businesses, too, are finding the same sense of bewilderment when dealing with the new grads. And the turnover has a huge impact on profitability. Bravo, Joanne and Jan!"

—Emil Scarano
President, Scarano, Trump, Adelsperger & Tucek

"When I started to read this book, I couldn't put it down. I know the importance of retaining high-performance employees who support patients and families at an extraordinary level of service. This book provides techniques and tools for understanding, managing, and keeping this talented generation—and others as well. Thanks Joanne and Jan for this outstanding contribution to the field of leadership and talent management."

—David Miles
CEO, The Children's Institute

"This book captures what I see in my Millennial teachers everyday. This generation is more flexible and adaptable to change. Every education administrator should read this book to help bridge the exceptional qualities and opportunities from all generations."

—Elle Parker
Principal, Cleveland Public Schools

"Ever wonder why many companies spend millions recruiting 20-somethings—only to ignore and alienate them once they're hired? If so, you'll welcome the thought-provoking answers, insights, and solutions provided in this page-turning book. The authors feature real-life examples from their years of consulting with top corporations to explain how to honor and integrate Millennials so they're contributing members of your work team. READ IT AND REAP."

—Sam Horn
International Communication Consultant and
author of *POP!* and *Tongue Fu!*

"This book describes what is really taking place in the corporate world! I am a Millennial who did find a job that challenges me, offers a flexible schedule, and gives me a chance to shine. My friends envy me because they didn't find what I have!"

—Ashley Willoughby
Paralegal, Ness USA, Inc.

"As the parent of a 21-year-old daughter, I found myself nodding in agreement as I read the on-target observations about her generation in *Keeping the Millennials*. But what really made the book helpful were the explanations behind the observations that allowed me to see these kids in a different light and understand why they do the things they do."

—Bill Koch
Cincinnati Enquirer sports reporter

KEEPING THE MILLENNIALS

WHY COMPANIES ARE LOSING BILLIONS IN TURNOVER TO THIS GENERATION— AND WHAT TO DO ABOUT IT

JOANNE G. SUJANSKY, PhD

JAN FERRI-REED, PhD

John Wiley & Sons, Inc.

Published by John Wiley & Sons, Inc., Hoboken, New Jersey.

Published simultaneously in Canada.

For general information on our other products and services or for technical support, please contact our Customer Care Department within the United States at (800) 762-2974, outside the United States at (317) 572-3993, or fax (317) 572-4002.

Wiley also publishes its books in a variety of electronic formats. Some content that appears in print may not be available in electronic books. For more information about Wiley products, visit our web site at www.wiley.com.

Library of Congress Cataloging-in-Publication Data:

Sujansky, Joanne Genova.
    Keeping the millennials : why companies are losing billions in turnover to this generation—and what to do about it / Joanne G. Sujansky, and Jan Ferri-Reed. p. cm.
    Includes bibliographical references and index.
    ISBN 978-0-470-43851-0 (cloth)
        1. Personnel management—United States.   2. Generation Y—Employment—United States.   3. Young adults—Employment—United States.   4. Employee motivation—United States.   5. Labor turnover—United States.   I. Ferri-Reed, Jan, 1953-   II. Title.
HF5549.2.U5S94 2009
658.3'01—dc22
                                                        2008055224

10 9 8 7 6 5 4 3 2 1

We dedicate this book to our fathers,
John W. Genova and Nick L. Ferri, both deceased,
and to our mothers, Mary Ellen (Mandarino)
Genova and Gloria (Ianotta) Ferri. These two
wonderful sets of parents, all from the Mature
generation, helped to make us who we are. We are
forever grateful for their love and support.

Contents

Acknowledgments

We have dedicated our business lives to making workplaces more productive and helping leaders motivate and retain their best talent. It was very important to us to make the business case regarding the Millennials. In every country that we've worked (more than 35) and every business we've consulted, there are multigenerational conflicts, amplified by the entrance of the Millennials. We are grateful to Matt Holt and Lauren Lynch of John Wiley and Sons, Inc., for believing in us and the need for this book; and to Sam Horn, who facilitated the KEYGroup® team's brainstorming session where the idea for the book was created.

Our KEYGroup team, most especially Kelly Hanna, Sandy Brown, and Patti Dubbs, were with us every step of the way: Kelly, for helping us to balance the writing of the book and our client work, and for her work in the wee hours of the night, recommending content and editing; Sandy, for her work on the manuscript and her continual encouragement; and Patti, for her research and editing. We love the illustrations done by our talented Millennial colleague Thomas J. Erny Jr. (www.thomasernydesign.com), who wishes to dedicate this work to his late grandfather, William Erny, who never really got to see his grandson's artistic abilities.

We thank our spouses, Chuck Sujansky and Rich Reed, for reminding us continually that our goal was a "best seller," and our Millennial children: Cara Olshanski; Justin Sujansky, who was an early, primary contributor; Jenna Sujansky; and Derek Reed, who challenged us to get it right.

Our greatest thanks goes to David G. Young, who was on the project from the beginning—researching, editing, and in fact managing the entire manuscript. We would recommend David to any serious authors in need of support throughout their writing process.

KEEPING THE MILLENNIALS

1

A Generational Battle Ahead

That which seems the height of absurdity in one generation often becomes the height of wisdom in another.

—Adlai Stevenson

There's a generational tidal wave coming that's threatening to shake up workplaces throughout the world. A new group is leaving college and joining the workforce in growing numbers. Sometimes referred to as "Generation Y," Millennials are the children of the vast "Baby Boomer generation." Born between 1980 and 1999, the "Millennial generation" is nearly as large a cohort as the Boomers. And as they take their places in the cubicles next door to their predecessors, a pronounced culture clash is inevitable!

When a harried office manager recently announced to his team that an evening of overtime was going to be required in order to finish an important project, he expected to hear a general round of grumbling. But he was shocked when a new member of the team, a 22-year-old recent college graduate, told him he couldn't stay because he had concert tickets that evening.

One company's human-resources recruiter was a little surprised at the middle-aged man that showed up in front of her booth at the job fair, considering that the fair was targeted to recent college grads.

1

But his purpose became clear a minute later when he introduced the young woman next to him as his daughter, a recent graduate who was considering her career options. The father spent the next 20 minutes asking questions on his daughter's behalf while she listened silently.

One of the directors of a midsize electronics company felt disheartened as one of the organization's most promising young fast-track employees left his office. The young woman had just turned in her resignation after little more than a year with the company. The director had listened to her carefully before laying out a case for why she should reconsider and stay with his firm. He discussed career advancement and exciting new projects. He even hinted that a salary increase might be arranged. But at the end of the interview, he simply couldn't counter her deepest desire, which was to become an entrepreneur and start her own company at the tender age of 27.

The hiring manager at a large retail chain was fuming when a coworker stepped into her office. She had just finished interviewing a young man for a new sales associate position at the store. The interview went well, but she was quite annoyed to receive a thank-you text-messaged from the candidate's cell phone to her cell phone not more than 30 minutes later. "I can't believe he had the nerve to send me a text message rather than a proper thank-you letter," she complained. Her coworker replied, "But he observed the courtesy of thanking you, and he probably figured it was both faster and more economical."

A retirement party for a department supervisor at one company was barely getting under way when one of the younger employees stepped up to the division manager and asked to be considered as the replacement for the departing supervisor. The manager was flabbergasted at the youth's nerve and self-confidence. After listening to a litany of reasons why the 25-year-old would make a good replacement for the department supervisor, the division manager became irritated. He asked, "Don't you think you're just a little young for that job?" The employee asked back, "What does age have to do with it?"

There's an invasion quietly taking place in organizations around the world. It's a revolution with the potential to forever change the way most workplaces function. It also brings with it prospects for new conflicts, as the members of one generation begin to work alongside the members of three older generations.

The Millennials are coming. They're well educated, skilled in technology, and very self-confident. They bring with them to the workplace high accomplishments and even higher expectations.

As the Millennials join the workforce, organizations are finding that their existing employees and managers are often befuddled and confused in trying to understand how the younger generation thinks and acts. Their behavior, their clothes, and their attitudes are becoming subject to scrutiny as they clash with existing corporate cultures.

Millennials will bring a new style and a new perspective to the workforce, but unless organizations are willing to adapt, they risk losing billions of dollars to unwanted turnover and lost productivity.

Smart gamblers play the odds and don't leave money on the table. Corporations would do well to take a lesson from them, because right now, the odds are stacked against most organizations. Too many of them are parting with money they can't afford to waste by ignoring some of the most promising employees ever to show up for interviews—Millennials.

Also known as "Echo Boomers," "Nexters," and "Gen Ys," most companies are playing a losing hand when it comes to employing these young people. And unless something radically changes, companies will continue to lose billions of dollars because they lack a process to attract, hire, and retain this dynamic new generation.

The Coming Tidal Wave

Millennials are moving into the workforce in big numbers, and the need to keep them there is even greater. The U.S. Bureau of Labor Statistics predicts a slowdown in the pace of labor-force growth and productivity in 2016, as some of the 70 million-plus Baby Boomers retire.[1]

And the escalating departure of Baby Boomers from the workforce represents only one facet of the problem. Currently, in the United States alone, about 40 million Millennials make a living in corporations. By 2014, their numbers will climb to about 58 million.[2] Not only are they a growing force in the workplace to be reckoned with, but reducing their turnover is also sure to become a major focus in the years ahead.

In addition, the Boomers are leaving a workplace that has been designed around them, which is now at odds with the work expectations of the Millennials who will replace them. The clash of workplace cultures is creating puzzlement, consternation, and havoc at companies that now find themselves faced with the need to adapt their cultures to the work styles of Millennials.

The other problem companies face is that Millennials are difficult to attract and once hired, don't stay around long. For many, their per-job tenure maxes out at two to five years. And some may not work for corporations at all, but will go into business for themselves instead. According to the OPEN Ages survey from American Express, Millennials are almost twice as likely as Baby Boomer small-business owners (59 percent versus 33 percent) to be or plan to be "serial entrepreneurs," owning or planning to own more than one business.[3]

All of this does not bode well for corporations. Unless companies find ways to attract Millennials more effectively—and to resolve their short job tenure—the turnover problem will continue to cost companies dearly. Turnover costs can easily range from 50 to 150 percent of an employee's salary.

But all is not lost. Cutting employee turnover can reduce these costs substantially. Let's assume that the average salary in a company is $50,000 per year, with a cost of turnover at 50 percent of salary. Therefore, the average cost of turnover is $25,000 per year per employee who leaves the company.

If a company employs 20,000 and experiences an annual turnover of 10 percent, the annual cost of turnover is $50 million. By reducing turnover by just 3 percent, the company can save $15 million annually.

Boomers versus Millennials

Millennial turnover is high for a number of reasons. Millennials move fast and want to be challenged. If they become bored in a job that fails to demand their best for long periods of time, they're gone. What's more, they're not loyal to their employers, as their Baby Boomer parents were. Millennials are loyal to people, however, so manager and peer relationships are important.

And the prospect of switching jobs isn't at all daunting to Millennials. Most of them expect to have an easy time finding employment. According to one Australian study, 52.3 percent of Millennials stated that it was currently "easy" or "very easy" to get a new job, compared to 43 percent of the Baby Boomers surveyed.[4]

Another challenge for companies employing Millennials is addressing the need for work–life balance. Baby Boomers have historically been willing to work 50, 60, or 70 hours a week to get the job done, often to the dismay and displeasure of their family and friends. Over time, as job security dwindled and the apparent rewards of workaholism faded, Boomers began to question that sense of unbridled dedication. In a 2006 KEYGroup survey that included 1,727 responses from multiple generations, one in every five indicated that they were planning to leave their jobs due to work–life imbalance.

Work–life balance means just as much, if not more, to the Millennial generation than it did to their predecessors. To some Millennials, it may even mean more than salary.

Author Morris Massey once said, "What you are is where you were when." His popular video series portrayed the differences between generations by focusing on the significant emotional events that influenced different generations during their "coming of age years."[5]

The Boomers grew up in an era of social revolution and widespread turmoil. The Cold War, civil rights, the peace movement, Vietnam, women's liberation, and similar events defined that generation. They entered the workforce in massive numbers and felt propelled to establish their careers. Like the generation before them, they played by the rules (for the most part)—marrying, starting families, and working their way up the social ladder. They entered the workforce secure in the belief that they could expect to enjoy a long, prosperous career and a happy, generous retirement.

In contrast, the Boomers' children grew up in a different revolution. The early 1980s saw an explosion of technology that transformed the fabric of our global society. Computers went from being a rarity in the office to being ubiquitous both at home and at work. Voice mail and cell phones permanently altered communication patterns, and video games changed the landscape of childhood. Even that mainstay of the Boomer's childhoods—television—morphed into a cable-driven, 500-channel juggernaut that consumed ever more hours of childhood leisure time.

Given the differences between growing up in the 1950s and growing up in the 1980s, it's inevitable that the two generations approach work and life in very different ways. It is those contrasts that foreshadow conflict in the workplace in coming years. But some of the conflict can also be found in the overlap between the shared experiences of Millennials and Boomers.

Boomer Dedication and Millennial Angst

Looking closely at the Millennial generation, one can detect an underlying current of sadness about their childhoods. Some Millennials seem to possess a sense of regret over the absence of their Boomer parents from the life events that mattered most to them growing up.

Under the demands of work and looming deadlines, a great many Boomers were compelled to miss soccer matches, football games, family dinners, musical recitals, and even graduation ceremonies. Millennials have transposed this mourning into a passionate embrace of work-life balance. Their lifestyle plan includes none of the heavy devotion to work that their Boomer parents have lived by. Millennials seek a multidimensional life by satisfying themselves through their work and personal lives. They're responsible and dedicated, but they expect flexible work schedules that will enable them to lead fulfilling lives. They truly work to live rather than live to work.

"My parents did what was necessary for the times," claims one Millennial, "but I don't plan on sacrificing my personal life to the extent that they did for their jobs."

Millennials not only want greater work-life balance, but they also expect to proceed along their career paths more rapidly than their parents. They witnessed their mothers and fathers waiting for years on end to get the promotions they deserved. Millennials want promotions, too, but they want them now; not 5, 10, or 20 years from now.

But Boomer parents haven't been totally absent from the lives of their kids. Quite the opposite, they've made their parental presence felt through massive levels of nurturing, pampering, mentoring, and coaching, all to make their children the best in whatever they choose to do. Millennials bought into this gospel of being the best, but they've also grown up relying heavily on their parents for guidance and help in reaching decisions.

One Boomer (unmarried with no children) was appalled to hear that a colleague's wife, after spending days moving her child into college, stayed in a hotel room close to campus for a week after school started to make sure her daughter was okay.

A Millennial freshman had this to share:

I met Sarah at spring orientation and decided that we would be perfect roommates. We had a lot in common immediately. Over the summer,

I flew to Virginia to stay with her for a week and to prepare for moving day. We moved to North Carolina for school and were both excited. However, I was shocked when Sarah's mother drove several hours from Virginia to North Carolina each week to take Sarah shopping and to do her laundry and cleaning. And if this type of hovering wasn't bad enough, I soon noticed that Sarah's mother was cleaning my side of the room, too! She made our beds and organized desk drawers! When I confronted Sarah about this, she quietly apologized and moved to a new dorm the next day.

Reflecting on this heavy reliance on parents, Professor Richard Mullendore of the University of Georgia has referred to the ever-present cell phones as "the world's longest umbilical cord."[6]

One study shows that about one in every four Millennials consults his or her parents first when making employment decisions.[7] No wonder many Millennials reach the workplace expecting their bosses to anticipate their needs, just as their parents have done.

Even though they have had highly structured lives and accept the need for some structure in the workplace, their desire for freedom is more than Baby Boomers ever experienced at work. The classic nine-to-five work shift is viewed as a guiding framework for them, not as a schedule to be slavishly followed. They tend to blur the lines between work and play. For example, if a Millennial completes a project by late afternoon and nothing else is due, he or she will likely consider the rest of the afternoon as time to take care of personal concerns. This perspective on work time partly stems from a desire to improve on existing ways of doing things. They have no trouble trying to work in ways that are faster, better, and easier. And if that means freeing up their time for other things, so be it.

High Tech . . . High Touch

In his 1982 best seller, *MegaTrends*, author John Naisbitt wrote, "Whenever new technology is introduced into society, there must be a counterbalancing human response—that is, high touch—or the technology is rejected."[8] In many ways, Millennials are the living embodiment of that observation.

Their high comfort level with technology sets Millennials apart from their Boomer parents. Boomers grew up getting most of their information from television (all four channels) and their entertainment from 8-track tapes and board games. Millennials, on the other hand, have grown up surfing the Internet, listening to MP3s, living off cell phones, and communicating with peers through instant messaging and texting. And woe to those Boomer parents who haven't learned to text message. They may never know where their kids are or what they're doing.

According to a 2005 Kaiser Foundation study, Millennials spend 6.5 hours a day communicating through some kind of medium and manage to clock in 8.3 hours worth of media exposure. That's because they multitask among various media. The same study also showed that 26 percent of the time Millennials interact with media, they're using more than one medium at a time.[9]

Given their natural affinity for technology, Millennials at work expect to have the latest technology at their fingertips. Anything less simply won't do. This expectation extends to much more than the latest computers and includes PDAs, iPhones, and BlackBerrys.

The technology orientation of Millennials carries over into their job searching. They regard the Internet as a research destination where they can ferret out information on companies that catch their interest. They browse corporate web sites to learn about prospective employers and actively use job boards and social-networking sites such as LinkedIn, Facebook, Twitter, and MySpace—hence the need for companies to convey corporate brands on their web sites, and perhaps on other electronic venues that relate to social-responsibility values Millennials hold near and dear. But merely touting these values is not enough. Companies have to show that they follow through on what they claim to value.

Millennials look for companies that truly take an interest in their employees; companies whose leaders inspire and challenge them to grow, who create ways for them to use their talents and skills, and who provide them with the resources—technological and otherwise—to do their jobs and self-develop. Companies that address these issues on their web sites come out ahead in attracting Millennials.

Getting Off on the Right Foot

But attracting Millennials is just the first step. Next comes hiring. Though highly idealistic, Millennials approach hiring situations and job offers with an equally high degree of pragmatism. For starters, they seek what members of every other generation have wanted in their work lives. They want to be proud of the companies they work for and the work they're hired to do. They seek work that is meaningful to them and that enables them to learn and grow on the job. And even though they may be inexperienced in work matters and protocols, they want to be listened to, appreciated for who they are, and respected for what they contribute to the enterprise, even while at the entry level.

Our client, a large full-service bank, communicates with prospective management trainees through its high-touch recruiting program. This effort consists of a series of hiring events that take place a number of times throughout the year. After each event, the company stages a "Super Saturday," during which up to 40 job candidates interview with different bank executives to learn about the bank's culture. The result is an 85 percent acceptance rate on job offers to college graduates and a retention rate for the program of about 70 percent.

A large investment-management firm recruits college graduates to work as associate research analysts for two or three years to learn the business. The experience enables them to know the company culture firsthand and lays the groundwork for them to pursue a master's degree in business administration.

Companies that take Millennials seriously know they don't seem to have the steadfast loyalty that Baby Boomers demonstrated.

Millennials want more from the companies they join. Employees today need to have job responsibilities that interest them and a clear idea of how they can grow. Thus, the new face of loyalty relates directly to the need that Millennials have to know what their advancement potential is when they take a job.

To address this need, successful companies engage them in "career pathing" or "career laddering," formal processes that show employees what their career progression can look like—not only up, but also sideways. Career-planning processes are generally competency and performance based. Employees get to know what behaviors they need for each position within a company and what they need to do to advance themselves. Career-planning processes enable companies to engage and keep top talent in their organizations and emphasize available opportunities while adding to corporate competitive advantages.

Show Me the Money

Career aspirations are important to Millennials, but future advancement does not take the place of salary, which research has shown to be an important employment consideration to members of this generation. When it comes to salaries and benefits, Millennials live in the here and now when negotiating these practical realities.

In a 2008 survey conducted by KEYGroup's research team, 1,020 Millennial respondents listed health benefits as the most important determinant of an attractive workplace. This was followed by work-life balance, promotional opportunities, and then salary. Who would have thought?

To engage Millennials on a deeper level, however, companies need to offer them more than the typical benefits package. A $160 billion commercial bank–holding company offers new employees benefits that are far from typical. Its Emergency Assistance Fund pays employees up to $1,500 if they experience a tragic event that results in severe financial hardship. They also offer flextime, reduced work schedules, part-time schedules, job sharing, telecommuting, pet insurance, and financial help for childcare.

At one of our client companies, a health insurance firm, employees enjoy the free use of fitness centers and may participate in clinically-based health and wellness programs. If employees can't access the fitness centers, the company supplies incentives to join health centers located near where they live. These benefits, in conjunction with other benefits and work-life programs, help the company to hold employee turnover to between 8 and 10 percent.

Creating the Millennial-Friendly Workplace

After Millennials are on board, how can companies respond more effectively to them? Our experience and research have shown that companies that respond best to the workplace challenges presented by Millennials share certain characteristics. During the new-hire orientation, they conduct preengagement surveys and focus groups among the Millennials they bring on board. They often connect them to internal mentors from all generations that provide guidance to new hires throughout their tenure with the company. These companies also realize that Millennials bring to the workplace a number of traits that make them well suited to a global workforce, such as the high value they place on diversity.

Millennials see the world as a union of people and countries connected electronically and technologically 365 days a year, 24 hours a day, and 7 days a week. These companies see to it that Millennials complete a thorough and realistic onboarding process— an extended new-employee orientation process that attempts to socialize new hires, helping them to get more ingrained in the company rather than just giving them an eight-hour overload of company policies and procedures. Ideally, the new hires learn the requirements of their new positions and receive exposure to different parts of the organization. This is also the socialization or acculturation phase, and for Millennials, an important one. It's where they will begin to establish and develop their social and professional network within the company, which they place a very high value on. It is important to design onboarding programs so that they encourage such interaction.

Today, many companies know that one of their greatest challenges is blending Millennial and Baby Boomer work cultures. But the greater reality is that for the first time in history, the workplace now comprises four distinct generations—Matures, Baby Boomers, Generation X, and Millennials. Hence, a good first step is to establish a process that attracts and retains Millennials while engaging multiple generations in the workplace.

The "Mature" or "Silent generation," born between 1909 and 1945, displays a loyalty to the company that places duty before pleasure. Baby Boomers, born between 1946 and 1964, are known for being workaholics, for maintaining a love-hate relationship with authority, and for being extraordinarily idealistic and optimistic. Gen Xers, the Music Television (MTV) generation, came into the world between 1965 and 1979. They often demonstrate independence, are results oriented, and are known for their skepticism.

Savvy companies that want to be the best in the eyes of Millennials communicate corporate vision, emphasize respect for diversity, and provide challenging work in which they can make the best use of their individual skills and talents. In an open work environment like this, not only the Millennials but also the three other generations understand where their companies are headed.

In a similar vein, Millennials relate best to companies that provide opportunities for advancement, interesting work, and regular training. Many progressive companies now offer online career-progression platforms in which employees can map out their own careers. They can look at open positions, book-training seminars, and develop skills necessary to continue growing on the job.

Millennials also respond better to managers who can coach them and provide them with real-time feedback. When they don't get it quickly, they are often impatient and may aggressively seek it. Remember, to them, no news is bad news. Those autocratic performance appraisals that are reviewed once or twice a year, so familiar to Boomers and so distasteful, are passé. They don't work for anyone. In KEYGroup's 2006 survey of 1,727 multigenerational respondents, more than half of the respondents indicated that they get feedback less than one time per week. So, they want it, but they don't get it.

Millennials are hungry for mentoring and coaching and respond readily to spontaneous feedback in real time. Feedback in the now helps them to know what they're doing right and how to make corrections and improve. They want to be the best, and they don't want to waste time waiting months on end to find out how they're performing.

So, Millennials are going to bring their high expectations with them to the job interview, and only those companies and organizations that live up to those expectations will have a shot at getting the best and brightest. But in order to keep them on the job, those organizations are also going to have to pay attention to a broad array of factors—from salary and benefits to perks and facilities—to create the types of "cool" corporate cultures that build Millennial loyalty.

But first we have to address these questions: What do Millennials expect from organizations, and what exactly is it that makes an organization cool?

Keys to Chapter 1

- Born between 1980 and 1999, the "Millennial generation" is nearly as large a cohort as the Boomers. And as they take their places in the cubicles next door to their predecessors, a pronounced culture clash is inevitable!
- Millennials will bring a new style and a new perspective to the workforce, but unless organizations are willing to adapt,

they risk losing billions of dollars to unwanted turnover and lost productivity.

- The number of Millennials in the workplace will continue to rise.
- Millennials are more likely than Baby Boomers to own more than one business in their lifetime.
- Unless companies find ways to attract Millennials more effectively—and to resolve their short job tenure—the turnover problem will continue to cost companies dearly. Turnover costs can easily range from 50 to 150 percent of an employee's salary.
- Most Millennials expect to have an easy time finding employment.
- Millennials seek a multidimensional life by satisfying themselves through their work and personal lives. They're responsible and dedicated, but they expect flexible work schedules that will enable them to lead fulfilling lives.
- Millennials consult parents before making employment decisions.
- Millennials spend a lot of time interacting with media and using more than one medium at a time.
- Millennials browse corporate web sites to learn about prospective employers and actively use job boards and social-networking sites such as LinkedIn, Facebook, and MySpace.
- Successful companies engage Millennials in "career pathing" or "career laddering," formal processes that show employees what their career progression can look like—not only up, but also sideways.
- Millennials see the world as a union of people and countries connected electronically and technologically 365 days a year, 24 hours a day, and 7 days a week.
- For the first time in history, the workplace now comprises four distinct generations—Matures, Baby Boomers, Generation X, and Millennials.

- The "Mature" or "Silent generation," born between 1909 and 1945, displays a loyalty to the company that places duty before pleasure. Baby Boomers, born between 1946 and 1964, are known for being workaholics, for maintaining a love-hate relationship with authority, and for being extraordinarily idealistic and optimistic. Gen Xers, the MTV generation, came into the world between 1965 and 1979. They often demonstrate independence, are results oriented, and are known for their skepticism.

2

A Workforce to Reckon With

Choose a job you love and you will never have
to work a day in your life.

—Confucius

Here they come to a workplace near you. They're the Millennials. They portend a revolutionary transformation of the workplace. They are also the first group that can truly be called the "Technological generation." Like no generation before them, they grew up with sophisticated technology, and it has come to define their lives.

But that is not the only thing this upcoming generation will bring to the workplace. In many ways, they may be the best-educated generation ever. In contrast to their predecessors, they've spent, on average, more hours in the classroom and more days in school. They participated in after-school tutoring programs, along with untold numbers of enrichment and private-tutoring programs.

The Millennials are also the products of the most overinvolved parents in the history of parenting. Their Baby Boomer mothers and fathers have become famous for a parenting style that included heaps of praise and plenty of parental hovering, for which they've come to be nicknamed "helicopter" parents.

One thing is certain: The Millennials are bringing to the workplace a new type of work ethic and a very different perspective than that of their Baby Boomer parents.

To many Boomer managers, it often seems as though the Millennials have little to no work ethic at all. But nothing could be further from the truth. In fact, as well educated and technologically savvy as they are, Millennials simply don't look at the requirements of getting a job done in the same way.

When Baby Boomers complain that the Millennial set doesn't seem willing to put in the legendary 50 to 70 hour workweeks that Boomers were famous for, their children might just as likely reply, "Why does it take you so long to get your job done?"

The Millennials expect a workplace that caters to their needs and their sense of time. It isn't that they're not adaptable. It's just that they see the world of work in very different terms.

Managers, Check Your Attitudes at the Door

It's not surprising that Baby Boomer managers and coworkers often take a dim view of Millennials. When Boomers entered the workforce in the very late 1960s and early 1970s, they had a very different set of career expectations. Boomers, not unlike their parents, expected to sign on with a single company for life. They expected to rise up the corporate ladder and eventually retire with a fat pension.

Imagine the Boomers' shock when major economic shifts resulted in corporate consolidation, massive layoffs, and the complete reordering of the employment landscape.

The children of those Boomer parents (our Millennials) watched as mom and dad ended up having to move from job to job throughout their careers. Millennials learned an important lesson that their parents eventually came to understand: There is no reward for loyalty to a corporation. Even long-term Boomer employees and those with outstanding track records went on the chopping block when economic conditions forced cutbacks. As it turned out, the Boomers didn't end up working a lifetime for one company. They ended up shifting jobs and even tackling new careers as the economy continued to mutate.

So, it is no surprise that the Millennials take a very different view of their career expectations. They don't expect lifetime employment and don't necessarily expect company loyalty. Some writers refer to them as "free agents," and in many ways, that's how they see themselves. They expect that their talent and skills will carry them far, and they're not shy about sharing those expectations with bosses, starting day one on the job. The minute they feel that their employers may not be providing career opportunities, these younger employees are indeed very likely to jump ship. This, too, alienates many Boomer managers.

But it would be a mistake to write off the Millennials as arrogant as a whole. They may actually be the most productive, innovative generation in history. Their high confidence is justified in the level of education and technology they have been exposed to. They expect much from their employers in terms of position and opportunities because it's their mindset. They are always thinking about what's in it for them. And in some cases, it isn't actually a case of arrogance, so much as it is a matter of well-justified confidence.

A 2008 survey conducted by Twenge and Campbell found that recent high-school students are very self-confident, predicting that they will perform extremely well in important adult roles. Two-thirds of recent high-school students believe they will be "very good" workers, roughly equivalent to the top 20 percent of performance. Only half of their parents' generation predicted this. Additionally, half of recent high-school students believe they will be "very good" spouses and parents, while only one-third predicted this in the 1970s.[1]

As noted earlier, companies and organizations around the world run the risk of being left behind if they don't recognize the potential value of this generation. By failing to attract and retain talented

Millennials, these organizations are literally risking billions of dollars in lost revenues and potential profits. Sadly, the current evidence suggests that most companies haven't yet connected the dots.

Is Your Atmosphere Fun?

The Mature generation would *never* have considered the workplace to be a source of fun. Work was to be endured, not enjoyed. Boomers weren't much different in their expectations, but they at least demanded that the workplace adapt better to their needs. Flextime, maternity leave, casual Fridays, and work-at-home options are all Boomer inventions. Work may not have been fun, but at least the company was supportive.

Millennials, on the other hand, bring an entirely different concept of fun at work. And it begins with their workplace tools.

As the first generation to be raised with technology, Millennials relate technology first and foremost to feelings of pleasure and enjoyment. While their parents struggled with complicated spreadsheets and arcane computer terminology, their children were happily playing computer-based games. To Millennials, technology means Nintendo and PlayStation, *Super Mario Brothers* and *Quake,* Game Boys and iPods.

Not that Millennials are reluctant to use technology for actual work. Remember, throughout school they also used the Internet for research, Microsoft Word for term papers, and PowerPoint for book reports. They are accustomed to using the latest technology, and they fully expect it to be engaging and fast-paced, filled with energy and surprises. In other words—fun.

Likewise, when it comes to the workplace and work itself, Millennials fully expect to be engaged and busy. They also expect plenty of human interaction, including in their use of technology. Unlike their Boomer parents, for whom e-mail is nothing more than another overflowing in-basket, their children see the computer as a ubiquitous form of communication. E-mail, instant messaging, text messaging, and social-networking web sites are all familiar tools for the younger generation.

Based upon their orientation to fun and technology, we can draw certain conclusions. Managers need to consider ways in which they can create an environment on the job that is fast-paced, engaging, and enjoyable. Obviously, not all work is fun, and most jobs contain a necessary amount of drudgery. However, when you go to the trouble to create a fun atmosphere, you not only attract Millennials, but you also unleash their naturally high energy levels. Think of the Millennial mantra as "work hard, play hard."

Bringing more joy into the workplace can also go a long way to reduce stress and increase productivity. In fact, in the 1,727-respondent, 2006 KEYGroup survey, one in every five respondents indicated that their productivity suffered because the company caused unnecessary stress, such as unclear deadlines.

Many organizations are taking concrete steps to develop a high-energy, social work climate. In some cases, casual Fridays have been replaced with ice-cream socials or end-of-the-week happy hours.

Some offices have even been known to organize spontaneous Nerf fights or to arrange after-hours paintball contests, just to break the monotony and generate some energy. Not only are these fun activities, but they also prove to be excellent team-building strategies!

Increasingly, many organizations are also setting aside time to organize employee trips. These can include theatre and sporting events, as well as community trips to museums, landmarks, and historical sites. They are enjoyable, serve as a reward, and contribute to team building as a side benefit.

Some companies, such as Google, even install Napping Pods for the employees' onsite to ensure that their workforce is adequately rested. Scientific studies conducted by Takahashi & Arito show that a short nap midday can boost the productivity of employees.[2]

Another way that organizations are cultivating a fun, intense work atmosphere is by replacing Muzak with television. It may seem jarring to older workers, but many employers are placing televisions in common areas and break rooms. In some cases, they even position televisions throughout employee workspaces, making the office atmosphere more closely resemble a sports bar. Televisions, once a clear taboo in the workplace, are gaining new currency among employers who seek to create a kinetic sense of energy in the office.

There are several justifications for this strategy. "Muzak" (a term for background instrumental music) was once thought to induce calmness and enhance employee productivity. Calming it may have been, but Muzak's productivity-enhancing properties are questionable. Instead, corporations are making news broadcasts, sporting events, and even MTV available to employees in an attempt to make work more enjoyable.

Even though TV may be a distraction to some, Millennials are used to it. A 2008 Motorola survey of 1,200 Millennials from five countries in Europe and the Middle East found that not only do Millennials themselves engage with new technology, but they also actually influence their parents to do so, even if they don't live in their home.[3] They are the all-time multitasking champs, and they have rarely done anything in their lives—from homework to reading to conversing—without the background chatter of televisions, MP3 players, and other electronic distractions.

However, technology looms far more significantly to the Millennial set than as a mere backdrop. Technology is at the heart of the Millennial generation's work ethic.

It's Not Your Father's Meeting

How many times have many of us exited a corporate meeting after two hours, wishing we could somehow get that time back? It's ironic, but most employees and most employers complain about the lack of communication in the workplace. Yet at the same time, both managers and employees often express frustration over the futility of meetings without end (and seemingly without purpose).

Well, it shouldn't be surprising that Millennials find meetings no more interesting than the rest of us. But be that as it may, organizational meetings are a way of life and are not likely to go away altogether anytime soon. However, if we pay attention to the skill sets that Millennials bring to the workplace, we may actually find ourselves in fewer meetings while enjoying better communications.

Ironically, many of the technologies that so sharply define the Millennial generation aren't really new. They've actually been available to the Baby Boomer generation that preceded them in the workplace for quite a few years now. It's just that Baby Boomers haven't always taken to these communication technologies in large numbers.

One of the biggest differences between Boomers and Millennials may be in their reliance on virtual communications. Millennials seem to use virtual communication more often than Boomers, and we're starting to see their overdependence on it as opposed to in-person contact. However, one point should be noted right at the outset. There is a need in almost every business environment for person-to-person meetings. Certainly, employee relationships with their bosses demand it to some extent, and nearly all relationships with coworkers depend on it.

E-mail has already revolutionized employee communications. That fact won't differ for Millennials entering the workplace. Millennials, however, are far more enthusiastic about sending text messages or engaging in instant-messaging dialogs. Unlike e-mails, these are real-time communications that allow people to interact spontaneously, albeit with short blasts of messages.

So far, instantaneous-communication technologies have not become pervasive in the workplace, but you can expect to see their rise as more and more Millennials join the workforce. Ironically, these technologies might actually herald the decline of e-mail or voice mail if employees come to prefer instant communication to communication that is delayed.

Many Boomer parents already express their frustration with Millennials who, when they can't reach mom or dad by phone, choose not to leave a voice mail message. To Boomers, this is unfathomable. But Millennials just seem to dislike leaving messages (or listening to them). They figure that when your caller ID shows who called, you will simply hit redial and engage in a real-time conversation. Millennials just can't see the value of wasting time by leaving a message or retrieving one.

So, we may end up seeing the decline of voice mail, and perhaps to a lesser extent the decline of e-mail, but with a corresponding rise in text messaging and instant messaging.

We might add here the suspicion that the Millennial generation may well be the worst-spelling group of people in history. In addition to the *intentional* misspellings that are a necessary part of texting ("R U there?") and instant messaging, Millennials simply show little patience for spell-checking their communications. The essence of modern communication is speed, not accuracy. E–mail, instant messaging, and text messaging are all virtually instantaneous mediums, with no time to run a spell-check.

We will probably see a rise in the technology of videoconferencing, as well as in virtual meetings and online collaboration. Videoconferencing is certainly not a new technology, and there are many companies that use it extensively. But considering the depth of our technology, it's not a communication strategy that most organizations use to bring together widely dispersed work locations. You no longer require elaborate and expensive video equipment to join a large videoconference. Today, one need only be equipped with a computer or a laptop and use of Skype.

Similarly, we have long had the technology that would enable us to engage in online collaboration with other employees utilizing the Internet, along with computer-based voice and video. Software programs and services such as NetMeeting should make it very cost effective for employees spread out across the globe to work closely together to coordinate efforts or solve problems.

But again, these technologies have existed for many years but have not yet come into widespread use. Now along come the Millennials, who are both highly technological and very comfortable with virtual communications. The "Facebook generation" could well come to redefine the nature of work in both space and time.

Your father may have been content to attend weekly staff meetings and the occasional all-hands meeting once a month. The Millennials, however, will expect more immediate communication in real time, with the least amount of inconvenience (and boredom) possible. This could well end up being a "Brave New World" for networking.

Will You Be My Friend?

But speaking of networking, we should acknowledge that the Millennial generation has a very different view of networking, and specifically how to network, than their parents did. Millennials are inveterate "joiners" when it comes to online social networks. The Facebook phenomenon is a case in point.

Facebook was founded in 2004 by a student at Harvard University. The site was designed to provide a place for students to create profiles and visit other students' profiles to learn something about each other's interests and background. Each profile might contain information about favorite music, schools attended, classes taken, and other matters of personal interest. The intriguing concept was allowing visitors to "join" a person's profile by listing yourself as a friend (with corresponding links back to your own profile).

By 2008, after only four years of operation, Facebook yields more than 132 million visits a day! Its older competitor, MySpace, only attracts a mere 117 million visits! Although the founders of these popular sites have been challenged to find ways to earn money from this global phenomenon, it is readily evident that the Millennial generation loves the concept of social interaction taking place in a virtual environment.

Businesses have not been immune to the appeal of social-networking sites, either. Another more venerable social-networking site is LinkedIn, which in a manner of speaking is a Facebook- or MySpace-style site that is intended for business networking. While LinkedIn is not as large as the more popular sites for younger people, in its own way, it has been just as much a surging success.

Another social-networking site with immense popularity among young people is YouTube. This video-driven site is also only a few years old, yet its rapid rise to popularity led Internet search–giant Google to purchase the site for $1.65 billion in 2006. The videos that people post to YouTube are typically amateur and personal. Yet, many of the visitors post videos about their jobs, their companies, their services, or their products. While the principal thrust is not a social-networking web site for business use, YouTube has actually become a surprisingly powerful marketing tool and a very effective way to reach Millennials. For example, when a couple of Millennials alleged that they were victim to age discrimination on a Southwest Airline flight, Southwest posted the company's response on YouTube. Even political candidates are on YouTube.

There are two elements to Millennials' affinity for social net-working that organizational recruiters need to pay attention to. One is that social-networking sites provide recruiters a way to connect with potential employees. Not surprisingly, organizations are creat-ing presences on Facebook, MySpace, and other social-networking sites. Even YouTube is a source for recruiters to send a message about working for their company.

But in the real world (as opposed to the virtual world), the phe-nomenon of social networking among Millennials says something about their desire for socialization. While they can be quite content to engage in virtual human contact, at the end of the day—and most certainly at the end of the workweek—they're still looking for actual human contact.

That's why many organizations sponsor the aforementioned social events, such as ice-cream socials and Friday happy hours, as a way of allowing their employees to interact and build relationships.

While they may be masters of the virtual world of bits and bytes, the Millennial generation, like generations that preceded them, still depends upon face-to-face contact and human touch.

The Achievers

One thing that may separate the Millennials from the generations that came before them is the extent to which they have been nurtured. Their parents, the Baby Boomer generation, behaved very differently from the way *their* parents had treated them. The World War II generation had a tendency to practice the philosophies that children are "better seen than heard" and "spare the rod and spoil the child."

In reality, of course, most of the Mature generation provided an unprecedented level of material comfort to their children. Most of their offspring also enjoyed a level of education that previous generations could only dream about. But when the Boomers began having children of their own, they carried the challenge of parenting to an extreme (just as they carried most things to an extreme).

To Boomer parents, it wasn't just a question of their children being well fed, well clothed, and well educated. The Boomers wanted and expected their children to do better than they did. To that end, they pushed, pulled, cobbled, encouraged, bribed, and motivated their offspring to reach for the stars.

Boomers were extremely involved and busy parents. Despite typically being a two-income household, the Boomers chauffeured their kids *everywhere*, from school to after-school activities. They ushered the Millennials to Girl Scouts, Boy Scouts, church groups, traveling sports teams, tutoring centers, summer camps, and more.

And those summer camps were a far cry from the summer camps of the Boomers' youth, where lazy days were spent making leather wallets and paddling around the lake.

Summer camps in the Millennials' era began to specialize, offering a unique focus—camp by camp—on pursuits such as computers, space exploration, sports, performing arts, and a myriad of other avocations.

One of the overall results of this intense level of parental attention was that the Millennials grew up receiving lots and *lots* of feedback. They're used to higher levels of praise and encouragement than correction. Although they are often uncomfortable in the workplace if they don't receive lots of feedback, our experience has been that many struggle with corrective feedback.

Supervisors who have hired and trained younger employees are already seeing this. Annual performance reviews are inadequate to Millennials, who want real-time feedback and often prefer scheduled face time for performance discussions. It may seem like a lot of hand-holding, but it's a very effective way to get Millennials motivated and to keep them on track.

This is both a challenge and an opportunity to those who are charged with managing Millennials. For the average Millennial, feedback is indeed the "breakfast of champions." The use of positive reinforcement to shape behavior will need to become a standard practice (if it isn't already), because Millennials are unlikely to respond well to negative reinforcement or reprimands. Guidelines to help Millennials give and receive positive and corrective feedback follows on page 29.

And don't forget to provide feedback to them as they demonstrate leadership competencies on the job. A record-keeping format that works well also follows on page 29.

Another way that the Millennials' craving for feedback is showing up in modern organizations is through employee-recognition and incentive systems. In the old days, it used to be enough for employers to post goal-tracking charts on break-room walls and conduct simple awards ceremonies to herald employee achievements. Today, members of the younger generation look for greater evidence that their achievements are recognized.

Guidelines for Giving Feedback

1. Be specific.

2. Focus on performance.

3. Consider the needs of the receiver.

4. Focus on performance over which the receiver has control.

5. Give timely feedback.

6. Check for understanding.

7. Document discussion.

8. Watch absolute words, such as "always" and "never."

Record Keeping for Accomplishments

Write an "Emmy speech" for each employee, recognizing and acknowledging each one's contributions.

This is a person who demonstrates:

_____

_____

(identify a leadership competency or an admirable quality that this employee displays)

Who has achieved:

_____

(identify this employee's accomplishments)

_____

(Name of employee)

For one thing, the goals have to be tangible and readily measurable. Second, the rewards themselves need to be goods or services that the Millennials actually value. Gift certificates are fine, so long as they are to venues and events that Millennials deem cool. If the rewards for high achievement are quality merchandise, such as iPods, they have a much greater impact. It's not just the recognition itself that impresses Millennials. High-quality rewards send a message that their effort is truly valued, as are they.

Many employers have had a great deal of success creating incentive programs to reward employees, especially their Millennials, for completing a predetermined schedule of learning and development programs. Millennials tend to value education in any event, but providing recognition for accomplishing a learning plan really gets their attention. Some employers have even used a point system for completing training objectives that permitted their employees to pick and choose from a catalog of gifts. The custom nature of this type of reward is really appealing to young people.

Because Millennials place a great deal of value on collaboration, it's often equally effective to reward them for their efforts as part of a team. By defining team goals and setting up rewards for hitting benchmarks, completing the project can be more productive in the long run. It can certainly provide an opportunity to insert a little team building as well.

Recruiting Strategies for the Cool Crowd

Marketers have discovered that Millennials can be a very difficult market. They are known for having a short attention span. It's a great quality to possess when you're multitasking, but it's a bad characteristic for those trying to present a message. Couple that with the Millennials' ingrained distrust of hype and spin, and you have a recipe guaranteed to drive marketers crazy.

Over the years, however, a few organizations have learned some effective techniques for getting their message in front of Millennials and earning their trust. One of the secrets that successful marketers have discovered is that Millennials place a very high degree of trust in word-of-mouth communication. A suggestion or recommendation from one of their peers carries vastly more weight with Millennials than a ton of glossy advertisements.

Perhaps it was inevitable. No generation in history has been exposed to as much advertising and as many commercial messages as the Millennials have!

Further, they have grown up in an era in which reporting the news has been superseded by expressing opinions. Talking heads have given way to shouting faces. Sometimes it seems that facts are in short supply, but we seem to have no end of opinions. And not just on television.

Opinions abound on the Internet. Almost any product that you can buy on most web sites comes with a stack of reviews from other people who've purchased the product before you. Articles published on magazine or newspaper web sites are evaluated and commented on by readers. Blogs exist on almost any subject by the thousands, and each and every blog is accompanied by feedback and discussion. Needless to say, social-networking sites are filled with compendiums of likes, dislikes, recommendations, advice, and other forms of opinion.

Marketers have responded to this characteristic of the Millennial generation with creative and unusual marketing campaigns geared toward generating positive word-of-mouth messages about their products.

Shoemaker company Vans scored big with Millennials by sponsoring skateboard tours and the X Games competitions. Jones Soda reached Millennials where they lived by selling soft drinks in clothing and music stores, tattoo and piercing parlors, and sporting-equipment shops before hitting the mainstream of beverage distribution. The challenge for each company, it seems, is to find a way to make that connection with the younger generation. Millennials have to see a way in which they can identify with a company if an organization wants any chance of them becoming fully engaged, either as customers or employees.

Viral videos are a good example of how word-of-mouth messages can spread like wildfire among Millennials. The advent of YouTube and the proliferation of cell-phone cameras has led to an explosion of amateur videos on the Internet. Much of what you see on sites like YouTube also comes from clips, commercials, and old video recordings. But whatever the source, when a clip catches the fancy of Millennials, they quickly spread the word, and the video in question gets viewed millions of times.

Savvy marketers have figured out how to take advantage of that phenomenon by posting commercial messages cleverly designed to look like video shot by amateurs. Oddly enough, one would think that the Millennials would resent the fact that a popular clip is actually a commercial message. However, if it's well done—meaning truly clever and funny—the Millennials will forgive the commercial nature of the clip.

The meaning is clear. Marketers—including employment recruiters—have to use modern media in a clever way to attract the attention of Millennials. This would be especially true if your goal is to communicate that yours is a cool organization.

One organization, for example, distributed video cameras among its employees and invited them to make recordings of some of the fun things they got to do while performing their jobs. Those videos were then posted to YouTube, where visitors could get a real insider's look at work life within the organization: A very clever use of modern technology to attract the younger generation!

Keys to Chapter 2

- Boomers demanded that the workplace adapt better to their needs. Flextime, maternity leave, casual Fridays, and work-at-home options are all Boomer inventions.

- Millennials relate technology first and foremost to feelings of pleasure and enjoyment. To Millennials, technology means Nintendo and PlayStation, *Super Mario Brothers* and *Quake,* Game Boys and iPods.

- Millennials also used the Internet for research, Microsoft Word for term papers, and PowerPoint for book reports. They are accustomed to using the latest technology, and they fully expect it to be engaging and fast-paced, filled with energy and surprises.

- Millennials fully expect to be engaged and busy at work. They see the computer as a form of communication. E-mail, instant messaging, text messaging, and social-networking web sites are all familiar tools for this younger generation.

- Many organizations are taking concrete steps to develop a high-energy, social work climate. In some cases, casual Fridays have been replaced with themed Fridays, ice-cream socials, or end-of-the-week happy hours.

- Increasingly, many organizations are also organizing employee trips to theater and sporting events, as well as community trips to museums, landmarks, and historical sites. They serve as a reward and contribute to team building as a side benefit.

- Millennials are the all-time multitasking champs, and they have rarely done anything in their lives—from homework, to reading, to conversing—without the background chatter of televisions, MP3 players, and other electronic distractions.

- Instant-communication technologies have not become pervasive in the workplace, but you can expect to see their rise as more and more Millennials join the workforce.

- Social-networking sites provide recruiters a way to connect with potential employees. Organizations are creating presences on Facebook, MySpace, and other social-networking sites. Even YouTube is a source for recruiters to send a message about working for their company.

- One of the overall results of this intense level of parental attention was that the Millennials grew up receiving lots and *lots* of feedback. They're used to higher levels of praise and encouragement than correction.

- Many employers have had a great deal of success creating incentive programs to reward employees, especially their Millennials, for completing a predetermined schedule of learning and development programs.

- Because Millennials place a great deal of value on collaboration, it's often effective to reward them for their efforts as part of a team. By defining team goals and setting up rewards for hitting benchmarks, completing the project can be more productive in the long run.

- Millennials place a very high degree of trust in word-of-mouth communication. A suggestion or recommendation from one of their peers carries vastly more weight with Millennials than a ton of glossy advertisements.

- Millennials have to see a way in which they can identify with a company if an organization wants any chance of them becoming fully engaged, either as customers or employees.

- Viral videos are a good example of how word-of-mouth messages can spread like wildfire among Millennials. The advent of YouTube and the proliferation of cell-phone cameras has led to an explosion of amateur videos on the Internet.

- Marketers—including employment recruiters—have to use modern media in a clever way to attract the attention of Millennials. This would be especially true if your goal is to communicate that yours is a cool organization.

3

Attracting Millennials . . . The "Cool Factor"

> If I have the belief that I can do it, I shall surely acquire the capacity to do it even if I may not have it at the beginning.
>
> —Plato, *The Republic*

Millennials have high expectations. They expect to do well in whatever career path they choose to follow, and they expect to be appreciated for their efforts. They also expect the organization they work for to be a cool place to work. Of course, the word "cool" is somewhat elusive. What's cool to one person may be uncool to another person. To a certain extent, the quality of coolness is in the eye of the beholder. But among Millennials, there are some common perceptions and values that tend to define which employers are cool and which aren't. And as intangible as this may seem to be, it is possible for an organization to transform itself from a dull place to work into an employer of choice.

Do Today's Companies Get It?

Up to now, it appears that attracting the younger generation is challenging for today's organizations. One sometimes hears the excuse that there just isn't enough talent to go around. Nonsense! There's plenty of talent in this generation, although it may not be readily apparent to Baby Boomer managers. The other part of the equation is this question: What do Millennials expect from corporations' recruitment?

Many of the inducements that were commonplace to their parents' generation may not be as appealing to Millennials. The proverbial "golden handcuffs"—a combination of attractive salary and durable benefits—don't necessarily have curb appeal with younger people. Because many don't expect to work for a single organization over the course of their career, a 401(k) or company pension plan simply may not be enough to keep them loyal until retirement.

In addition, Boomer parents may have accepted working conditions as they were, even if facilities, technology, and work atmosphere were less than ideal. Not so for the Millennials! They bring with them to the job interview a keen sense that they are looking for the ideal work environment; one that meets their physical, intellectual, and social needs. And why not? Throughout their education, most have been catered to by grammar schools and universities that provided state-of-the-art technology, sophisticated modern sports equipment, and plenty of collaborative opportunities.

To simply plop Millennials into cubicles in front of obsolete computers and expect them to grind out an eight-hour day is an exercise in foolishness.

As one sales manager states:

I am very fond of the Millennial employees that are on my sales force. They bring fresh air to the team, and their outlooks are different. Most are used to getting everything they want and being invincible. The problem is, they don't deal well with adversity. They tend to move on if things become hard for them or if they are not moving up fast enough. They want to be a vice president by the time they reach 30 years old; millionaires by the time they reach 35 years old. They may spend three to four years learning this job, then they leave to pursue something cooler or sexier. I think that this generation needs to see more professional role models that aren't 35 years old and hot looking. They need to work with the dad that drives a van to work.

Another aspect of this generation that many employers don't seem to get is that Millennials expect to be fully involved with their managers. Baby Boomers may have tolerated occasional meetings and annual performance reviews with their bosses. Millennials are expecting frequent contact with their bosses, which includes lots of praise and an open exchange of ideas. Millennials are not at all shy about sharing their opinions, however new to the workplace they may be. And they expect those opinions to be taken seriously. Don't make the same mistake as one senior manager, who asked his team what could be improved on but did nothing with the feedback after team members candidly described issues and potential solutions.

All of this adds up to a potential problem for today's organizations when it comes to attracting and retaining Millennial employees. If companies don't make an effort to create the type of work climate that appeals to them, these organizations could find themselves in the shallow end of the talent pool in coming years!

The "Cool Factors"

Given the Millennials' high level of expectations, it's not surprising that they gravitate toward organizations that seem to cater to their needs, interests, and enthusiasms. These are the organizations that possess that elusive "cool factor." It's not always easy to determine what makes an organization cool. Retailers and advertisers, realizing the complexity of this task, have hired "cool hunters" to help them reach the teenage and young adult population. Employers would do well to better understand and attract this demographic.

Not all organizations shape up as cool—at least at first glance. Some may come to it more naturally, just by virtue of the work they do. Internet companies leap to mind. Other organizations may have to examine what they bring to the recruitment table and make some adjustments.

But first we have to ask: What exactly makes an organization cool?

That's what Wisconsin's *Small Business Times* wanted to know last year when they asked the 50 fastest-growing companies in southeastern Wisconsin, "What makes your company cool?" Some of the respondents talked about things like their corporate mission, generous benefits, or the products they produced; factors less likely to be looked at as cool. Others described creative communications to replace stale meetings, contests, employee-centered facilitation, and work flexibility. As one entertainment industry CEO put it, "Anyone can own equipment. It's the people that propel the business forward. Since we understand that, we embrace it and proactively focus on getting the right people on the team, getting them into the right positions, and keeping them challenged and satisfied in those positions."[1]

If there is a common theme to the perks that cool companies provide, it may be the message to employees that "you matter to us; your well-being, comfort, and enthusiasm are important to our success."

But these concepts aren't new. For several years now, recruiters have realized that cool corporate culture attracts Millennials. Organizations that possess this type of culture consistently demonstrate that they are ahead of the curve in a variety of ways. They demonstrate the ability to respond quickly to external demands, yet at the same time remain stable and viable in the long run. But coolness isn't something you can take for granted! History is littered with once-cool companies that took their ability to attract good talent for granted and now can't regain that cachet. For example, Lotus Development Corporation (creator of Lotus 123 software), Commodore International (makers of the once best-selling personal computer), and America Online were all considered to be *the* place to work at one time or another. Then, too late, they realized that all the great talent was going elsewhere.

So, what do Millennials find cool? The following list of ten cool factors was compiled from surveys of KEYGroup's interns over the last seven years, feedback from Millennials in our client companies, and focus groups we conducted at conferences and workshops:

- Fun work environment with social networking (see Chapter 2)
- Creative communications (see Chapter 2)
- Feedback and recognition (see Chapter 2)
- State-of-the-art technology
- Creative perks
- Corporate values
- Redesigned cubicle workspace
- Workplace flexibility
- Compensation and benefits
- Career development

But what can your company do to take advantage of these factors? Let's look at some of the options.

The Masters of Technology

For Baby Boomers, technology was always a bit of a love-hate matter. After all, personal computers were the creation of several renowned Baby Boomers, such as Bill Gates, Steve Jobs, Steve Wozniak, and Larry Ellison, to name just a few. However, their customers frequently found technology to be a mixed bag. In many ways it still is.

Those Boomers who've lived through the development of various personal computer operating systems, with all of the attending crashes, viruses, bugs, and other problems, know full well that the implementation of computer technology has been haphazard and often frustrating. Technology is great when it works and mind frazzling when it fails.

To Baby Boomers' children, however, modern technology has been a fact of life. In most parts of the world, by the time Millennials were entering school in 1988, personal computers were widespread and fairly reliable. Within 10 years, the framework that Millennials rely on today was pretty well established. As children, they were adventurous with gadgets and seldom afraid of crashing their computers or ruining their software. For the most part, technology just worked, and it proved to be the most highly interactive, engaging, exciting, and personally rewarding toy that any child has ever had to play with, perhaps in the entire history of childhood!

The Millennials played with technology, lived with it, worked with it, and learned from it. Gadgets of all sorts have been ever-constant companions to this generation, and the technology has shaped their thinking and values.

For example, it seems perfectly natural to them to have access to between 300 and 500 television channels, including a dozen news outlets. (Boomers, you may recall, grew up with four channels and a test pattern between midnight and the wee hours of the morning.) Is it any wonder that young people today are reading newspapers in ever-decreasing numbers?

Boomers considered themselves high tech when they gradually began adopting Palm Pilots (and similar devices) as a convenient way to keep themselves organized. Millennials, on the other hand, have adopted an entire host of technologies. Nintendo, iPods, and cell phones are nearly as necessary to Millennials as air, food, and water. Technology is always with these young people, and they can be found calling, texting, and listening to music no matter where they are. (Frequently, all at the same time.)

Consider music alone as a case in point. Music is an important experience for all teenagers. This has always been true. From Elvis Presley to Elvis Costello and from Chuck Berry to Buck Cherry, teenagers have always relied on music to express and understand their feelings.

So, when sharing music files across the Internet became popular back in the mid-1990s, Millennials embraced the practice in droves. The music industry hit the panic button and initiated a raft of lawsuits to prevent what it called "illegal downloading."

To Millennials, however, sharing music over the Internet was seen as a right, not a privilege (or a copyright). To them, the Internet was a vast, open playground in which information and files and pictures should all be free of charge. Granted, this appears to be a sense of entitlement, but Boomer managers need to be aware that it is exactly this same sense of entitlement that Millennials bring to the workplace, including their expectation to be armed with state-of-the-art technological tools.

Woe be to the organizations that take technology lightly. If they're interested in recruiting new talent among Millennials, they had first better make sure that their Internet presence is sophisticated and highly functional. Further, the savvier organizations are developing presences on popular web sites such as Facebook, MySpace, and YouTube, among others.

As far as the implementation of computer hardware, nothing less than the best will do to satisfy Millennials. Most already have top-of-the-line computers of their very own—most likely notebook computers. To saddle them with antiquated technology in the workplace is to send the message that the organization is not serious about the work. After all, why wouldn't you give them the tools to do the job that you've assigned them to perform?

When we were brought into a large financial institution to help with the retention of Millennials, we found from the focus groups we facilitated that the laptops and iPhones went entirely to the most senior staffers, presumably as a reward for long-term loyalty and seniority. But to the younger employees, it was evidence that they weren't taken seriously by management, especially considering that most of the people receiving the tools weren't technological and tended to use them as office decorations rather than as work tools!

In truth, there are many Boomer-run companies that almost seem computer-adverse, despite installing machines for nearly every employee. It is not uncommon to hear from employers that not all of their employees have access to computers. And worse, some Boomer managers are obsessed with preventing the supposed misuse of technology on the job. This has resulted in policies prohibiting personal e-mail, text messaging, general Internet usage, or playing games in the office. One large healthcare organization stopped providing iPods with procedural downloads to nurses because patients thought the nurses were listening to music rather than using them as a teaching resource.

A Millennial regional bank manager was using her personal BlackBerry to do her job because the bank disallowed Internet access. Her response? "My job is sales. How can I secure multimillion dollar business accounts if I can't research the company before I go on the sales call?"

These prohibitions are actually offensive to Millennials, especially when accompanied by secret surveillance of employees' computer use by the information technology department. Remember that Millennials are masterful multitaskers who really can conduct business while simultaneously surfing the net or instant messaging a friend.

This kind of management mindset is symptomatic of the obsolete policies of the past, when employees were expected to pay more attention to form rather than to function. It speaks of a time when people were paid by the hours they spent at work and not by the results they generated. Many managers have simply never been willing to trust that home-based employees were not watching reruns of *I Love Lucy* rather than handling customer service calls. Cool companies need to get serious about virtual work. An example of a company that makes this work is IBM, saving the corporation real-estate dollars for office space and saving employees commuting time and expenses.

This type of flexible thinking is simply aligned with the mindset of these young adults and should really be embraced by managers looking for a dynamic, creative workforce that can adapt to rapidly changing conditions. In other words—Millennials! They see the true power of technology and can't understand the attitude that these tools aren't to be trusted or fully used.

In fact, truly savvy managers at cool companies will find ways to harness all of the potential of technology to transform the workplace.

The Magic of Perks

Organizations have traditionally used perks to attract and retain the most talented employees. The word "perk" is a British term for "benefits in kind," originally called "perquisites" (otherwise perqs—or perks—for short). Perks are benefits such as health insurance, life insurance, day care, retirement benefits, tuition reimbursement, paid vacation, profit sharing, or other specialized goods or services. Increasingly, job candidates are beginning to look at perks as symbolic of the organization's commitment to a dynamic and high-energy work environment.

A recent and growing trend, for example, is the prevalence of on-site health facilities. Exercise equipment, jogging tracks, juice bars, and aerobics classes can be found in more and more organizations. Even that venerable perk—the employee cafeteria—has undergone a modern makeover. The old-fashioned tray-line cafeteria has been replaced by more contemporary forms of food service, such as Internet cafes and delis. And frequently, these on-site services open early and stay open late to accommodate long hours, late nights, weekends, and take-home meals.

Perks are simply another way for employers to send the message to employees that "we care about your comfort and convenience while you are working on our behalf." It's an important message for all of us, most importantly Millennials.

A Long Way from the United Way

It's a very common expectation that most organizations devote some percentage of their revenue and efforts to charitable activities. It's considered to be part of the social responsibility of companies that benefit from trading in the commercial marketplace. For the most part, employees of these companies are rightfully proud of the role their employer takes in making the world a better place. But until recently, that role was fulfilled in a relatively passive manner. No longer.

Typical of the old paradigm for corporate charity was the classic United Way campaign. United Way, representing a basket of charities, was traditionally a very appealing choice to direct organizational fund-raising. The typical United Way campaign matched voluntary employee contributions with corporate contributions. A convenient payroll deduction program made it easy for companies and employees alike to make reasonable donations to a worthwhile cause. Couple that with a smidgen of competitiveness, and each organization's United Way campaign was a chance to show a little corporate and personal charity.

However, this is not the type of charitable effort that Millennials find appealing. The younger generation prefers a more hands-on, personal, and direct approach to charity. Fortunately, many organizations have already followed this approach to volunteerism.

One way to energize employees around social causes is to allow them to select the charity of their choice and form a fund-raising team to raise money for their worthy cause. In some cases, these teams simply perform activities to raise money, such as special events to encourage contributions.

But it isn't uncommon to see employee teams given a release from a day of work in order to paint houses, pick up litter, construct new facilities, or just generally engage in some "do gooding." Scout around a few corporate web sites these days, and you'll find detailed stories about how many hours employees volunteered over the last year.

Why does this matter? To Millennials, an organization's charitable profile tells them something about the organization's values. These young people want to align themselves with the type of company that makes them feel proud—a company that's involved in the community and that values volunteerism.

Remember, most of these children were raised in an environment in which they were required to contribute service to the community. This wasn't just a casual expectation. In some places, student community service was considered an essential factor in receiving the credentials necessary to graduate from secondary school.

But another factor often overlooked when talking about Millennials is that, as the sons and daughters of the Baby Boomer generation, they received a dose of idealism along with their baby bottles. Arguably, the Boomer generation never quite lived up to its ideals from the late 1960s and early 1970s, but that doesn't mean Boomers didn't share those ideals with their offspring. The possibility, of course, is that their children actually may end up realizing some of the vision of the song "Age of Aquarius" from the musical *Hair* (released by the musical group Fifth Dimension in 1969), which seems to have been lost so long ago.

Another way in which they evaluate the social conscience of an organization is to look at the core values that each corporation espouses. Millennials want to join a company at which the competitive vision and social compass are aligned. Take Bank of America, for example. Its new building in New York is one of the greenest buildings in the city. Over time, it will also provide the bank an economic advantage from an energy standpoint. Millennials are attracted to companies that can think ahead like that.

These ideals certainly differ from organization to organization. But what they share is the power to convey a vision and a sense of shared direction that Millennials typically find inspiring. For example, the core values of Whole Foods, an upscale, organic grocery chain, sets the mark for coolness when it comes to vision.

Whole Foods' motto is, "Whole foods, whole people, whole planet." Whole Foods' vision is set forth on its web site and displayed prominently in all of its stores. The company's values encompass its commitment to quality products, customers, communities, and the environment.

Whole Foods goes beyond the traditional mechanics, such as work objectives and mission and vision statements, explaining exactly why the organization does what it does. Core-values statements like this seem to quicken the pulse of Millennial candidates and inspire them to want to get on board!

Also consider Zappos, an online customer-centric business that has grown exponentially since its shoe-sales inception in 1999. Core values, listed on its web site, make clear that its fun, team-based workplace exists to wow customers with such exceptional service and selection that the company couldn't justify shopping anywhere else. What a great service to customers, and what a sure fit for Millennial workers.

So, if you have a set of core values, be sure to trumpet them in all your recruiting efforts. If your organization is lacking a core-values statement, it may be time to address what the organization stands for.

A New Look for the Old "Cubicle Farm"

The migration of Baby Boomers from the classroom to the office in the late 1960s coincided roughly with the introduction of cubicles into the workspace. Prior to then, most office layouts featured managers' offices aligned along the outer perimeter, surrounding a sea of desks, neatly arranged row by row in the middle.

If workers of that era had any doubts about their lowly status, it surely had to have been confirmed by the regimentation, drabness, and lack of privacy they experienced putting in an eight-hour day in close proximity to a small army of other clerks and workers. Eventually, it became apparent to office designers that this type of office layout was far from conducive to high productivity and employee morale.

Workers were finally given a degree of privacy (and a touch of their dignity back) when office designers began to introduce cubicles in the early 1970s. At the time, this change was greeted as a virtual revolution in workplace climate. The cubicles were soundproofed to an extent, and workers were permitted, in most cases, to decorate them as they pleased. There can be little doubt that the advent of cubicles was, in fact, a major step forward.

The drawback became apparent, however, some years later when employers began to realize that cubicle farms had a tendency to inhibit collaboration and teamwork. The very name "cubicle farm" (a term popularized by Scott Adams, the creator of the *Dilbert* comic strip) demonstrates the feelings of distaste office workers have for this type of layout.

It doesn't appear that these cubicles are going away any time soon. But office designers are beginning to realize that steps can be taken to make the work environment more conducive to collaboration and more energized in an effort to appeal to younger workers. This is already showing up in workspaces designed around open collaborative areas. Managers are beginning to realize that Millennials spent a lot of time working collaboratively throughout school and college. They're the generation that tends to do everything in groups. Growing up, they played numerous team sports, they went out on group dates, and they were assigned plenty of group projects by their teachers. That's why those managing younger workers frequently find it more productive to assign them to team projects and workspaces where they can freely brainstorm and collaborate. Old-fashioned, large conference rooms are giving way to many open workspaces scattered throughout the floor, along with smaller private work stations that employees can opt into. At one investment firm, employees were experiencing difficulty communicating because of the physical layout. In order to physically talk to each other, they would have to get on an elevator and take it to one of the six floors in the company. To solve this problem, the firm installed spiral staircases in the middle of the working floors, giving employees easy accessibility to travel from floor to floor and enhancing collaboration between groups.

Greenery also seems to be making a big comeback, as designers are attempting to give office complexes a more natural feeling. Combined with vibrant wall color and touches of media, such as flat screen TVs fixed to some of the walls, it'll be the kind of charged atmosphere that younger, multitasking employees find energizing. Our client, GlaxoSmithKline, is providing its brand teams with vibrant, team-focused workspaces where all technological devices are mobile. It will be an atmosphere that encourages more open communication, both face-to-face and among groups.

Millennials are not going to lose their "herd instinct" at work, nor their high-energy multitasking. That's why modern office spaces have to be redesigned to consider their needs and strengths.

A New Take on Flextime

The drudgery of corporate life is well depicted in movie cult classics such as *Office Space* and *Clockwatchers*. *Office Space* highlights the miserable life of a cubicle-imprisoned software engineer who is challenged with incompetent managers, inane coworkers, and a morale-challenged work environment focused on minutia and mediocre performance at best. *Clockwatchers* portrays an organization in which almost every employee spends the day desperately trying to fill time until the work shift is over. If *Office Space* and *Clockwatchers* represent the way typical Millennials view office work, then who could doubt that they would rather be out paintballing than completing budget reports (referred to as test procedure specification [TPS] reports in *Office Space*).

Most modern organizations have moved past the paradigm of paying workers just for punching in and punching out. A few businesses have implemented creative approaches involving pay-for-performance and incentive-pay programs, but unfortunately, some workers themselves cling to the notion that all they are being paid for is the use of their time.

It certainly seems that way to Millennials. Even though most progressive companies offer generous vacation and personal time, Millennials, far more than previous generations, tend to see their time as their own and not the property of their employer. This perspective causes some of the biggest conflicts between them and Baby Boomer bosses.

Boomers often complain that Millennials just don't have the same work ethic as they do. Well guess what? They don't! This doesn't mean they don't have as good of a work ethic. It just means that they have a different work ethic than their parents.

Millennials expect to be paid for their talents and their contributions and do not favor the traditional workweek as most of us know it. Most don't see the point of being paid just for putting in time. Millennials view the use of their time on the job as no different than their time spent off the job in more interesting pursuits. And they want flexibility and control over both.

At KEYGroup, we employ Millennials for various assignments, including graphic-arts work for marketing and course workbooks. One of our young men, who holds a full-time job and does work like ours on the side, caught a heavy-duty flu bug and missed two days with his full-time employer. He made up those days the following weekend and completed our project on time. We had a good chuckle, as the project involved an article that discussed their need to "have a life," but their willingness to "burn the midnight oil" when necessary.

Boomers, after all, were always counted on to put the job first. The Millennials remember this, too. For many of the younger generation, mom and dad always seemed to be working, bringing work home, putting in long days, and working over the occasional weekend. Millennials recall that those kinds of hours didn't make mom and dad any happier. And workaholism didn't pay off when mom or dad ended up losing that job to a force reduction or merger!

So to Millennials, it only seems natural to consider leisure time just as important as work time. That doesn't mean they're not motivated. In the right circumstances, the younger generation can and will work relentlessly. They just have to be managed in the right way. But how?

For starters, managers need to remember that flexible hours loom very large to Millennials. They become frustrated at the notion of being bound to a computer, a desk, or a cubicle. They will certainly respect deadlines, so long as the deadlines are made clear to them and they have some role in negotiating them. Provide them with a little understanding that their personal time is their personal time, and you'll gain their enthusiastic support for your goals.

More significantly, it's important for managers to make it very clear to their younger employees the concrete results expected from them. KEYGroup's 2006 survey revealed that only 47 percent of the 1,727 multigenerational respondents were given clearly defined goals for their jobs. Since Millennials are far more results-oriented than time-oriented, some companies have changed their practices. Much has been written about Best Buy, an electronics company that has made gains in productivity and engagement due to a shift to a results-oriented environment. The results focus is based on judging performance on output instead of hours and face time.

In a Xerox-commissioned online survey of 1,250 executives in 16 countries in Europe conducted by Forrester Consulting, Sun Microsystems reported that it saved an estimated $63.8 million in office and property costs in the 2005 fiscal year by implementing a flexible work program. Also, AT&T employees gained an additional productive hour daily due to its work-at-home program.[2] In the long run, companies that set measurable, outcome-based goals will most likely find higher-performing, more satisfied employees and bottom-line gains.

Although Millennials blur the lines between work and personal time, changed deadlines, last-minute work assignments, or unexpected problems are a different matter and will certainly dampen their enthusiasm—you'll risk losing them.

In these circumstances, their view is likely to be, "It's not my fault you couldn't manage your project properly!" Boomers may have been more tolerant of these situations. But for most Millennials, life comes first for them—not work—and when their personal time is respected, the Millennials will show gratitude and give you their best efforts.

But there are also other traditional issues that affect Millennials deeply.

The Price Is Right

Salary is certainly not the sole motivator for Millennials, which the 2008 international KEYGroup survey revealed. It ranked fourth among the 21 choices offered, preceded by health benefits, work-life balance, and promotional opportunities.

Millennials *do* understand what's important in today's world. The things they like to do, the products they like to buy, and the sports they like to engage in all cost a lot of money. They expect to be well paid for their talents, and many recruiters often find their compensation expectations to be surprising, if not breathtaking.

On a final note, don't expect Millennials to keep salary figures confidential. They won't. This is a generation that shares information over the Internet freely and without reservation. They don't have the same traditional notions of privacy, and they don't consider the question of how much money others make to be a private matter. They will freely discuss how much they earn with friends and coworkers.

Hiking the Career Path

Much is made of the notion that Millennial job candidates are not destined to become long-term employees. They've been nicknamed "free agents" precisely because people expect them to offer themselves to the highest bidder, career prospects aside. But these young people don't differ that much from their predecessors in their desire to rise up the corporate ladder.

And with all of the skills, talents, and education they bring to the party, many of them expect to go far and fast. The key to managing Millennials' aspirations is their deep desire for appreciation. Frequent, positive feedback is the best way to harness their energy and enthusiasm. But it's also important to show them how their contributions fit into the big picture. They want to know that their success and progress are directly related to their efforts.

In contrast, if you want to know how to lose a Millennial, just wait 18 months and then conduct the traditional yearly performance review. Their Boomer parents probably wouldn't have complained much about the delay as long as the raise was retroactive, nor would they have expected anything but an appraisal form—subjective in nature and not future-focused.

You can expect the Millennials to take any delay in their review as negative feedback. They tend to take these things personally, and if you hold off giving them feedback, it just confirms suspicions that you don't take them seriously or value their efforts. They expect to have their achievement recognized and to have some discussion about how they can do better.

Also, you should take pains to discuss potential career paths with your Millennial employees. It's a cinch they don't plan on doing the same work for years on end. Their boredom threshold is way too low for that. So, make sure they understand that there are different assignments and career-path alternatives ahead of them as they progress within the organization.

And don't forget to factor in the prospects of special assignments and ad hoc task teams. Millennials tend to view assignments like this as recognition of their abilities and accomplishments.

Earlier generations often took a dim view of special work assignments. We've all suspected that the reward for hard work is more work! But to Millennials, special assignments are more than a refreshing break in routine. They tend to see them as a special recognition of their talents.

Millennials feel the same way about routine promotions. They're not averse to paying their dues the same way as previous generations, but the sense of entitlement they bring to the workplace means that they expect to be promoted when they are ready, not when they are tenured enough. In their minds, they're not troubled by questions of age, length of service, or position.

When a Millennial is ready to take on the job of team leader or supervisor, it doesn't occur to him or her that older, more tenured workers may be uncomfortable or resentful. That's because Millennials haven't been exposed to the same pecking order that older generations have experienced.

The first jobs for millions of Millennials have been in the fast-food industry, where older workers might find themselves reporting to a much younger shift supervisor. The same phenomenon has been found in retail chains, such as electronics stores, where younger workers are supervising older employees. This is a circumstance that would have been extremely rare in the younger years of the Baby Boomer generation.

So, Millennials may not be as hung up on hierarchy and social status as previous generations may have been. In their view, if they qualify for a promotion, what other dues should they have to pay? Recruiters looking to attract younger employees may want to stress the type of promotion opportunities that exist in their organization, regardless of age or tenure. Millennials are interested in promotions based on merit rather than on longevity.

And if you are in the business of recruiting Millennials, beware of the buyer's market for new employees in the coming years. With Boomers retiring in droves during the next two decades, their children have ample opportunities to pick and choose the jobs that they find most appealing. It's already been established that loyalty is not a high expectation among Millennials, so you can't expect them to cling to the job merely out of a sense of obligation or gratitude. The rungs on your organization's career ladder had better be solid!

Keys to Chapter 3

- Millennials have high expectations. They expect to do well in whatever career path they choose to follow, and they expect to be appreciated for their efforts.
- Many of the inducements that were commonplace to their parents' generation may not be as appealing to Millennials. The proverbial "golden handcuffs"—a combination of attractive salary and durable benefits—don't necessarily have curb appeal with all younger people.
- Millennials are not at all shy about sharing their opinions, however new to the workplace they may be. And they expect those opinions to be taken seriously.
- If there is a common theme to the perks that cool companies provide, it may be the message to employees that "you matter to us; your well-being, comfort, and enthusiasm are important to our success."
- A list of ten cool factors was compiled from surveys done by KEYGroup and includes: (1) fun work environment with social networking; (2) creative communications; (3) feedback and recognition; (4) state-of-the-art technology; (5) creative perks; (6) corporate values; (7) redesigned cubicle workspace; (8) workplace flexibility; (9) compensation and benefits; and (10) career development.
- Companies interested in recruiting new talent among Millennials had first better make sure that their Internet presence is sophisticated and highly functional.
- Increasingly, job candidates are beginning to look at perks as symbolic of the organization's commitment to a dynamic and high-energy work environment.

- Perks are simply another way for employers to send the message to employees that "we care about your comfort and convenience while you are working on our behalf." It's an important message for all of us, most importantly Millennials.

- To Millennials, an organization's charitable profile tells them something about the organization's values. These young people want to align themselves with the type of company that makes them feel proud—a company that's involved in the community and that values volunteerism.

- Millennials want to join a company at which the competitive vision and social compass are aligned.

- Office designers are beginning to realize that steps can be taken to make the work environment more conducive to collaboration and more energized in an effort to appeal to younger workers. This is already showing up in workspaces designed around open collaborative areas.

- Millennials tend to be more results-oriented than time-oriented.

- Flexible work programs can increase productivity and reduce costs.

- The key to managing Millennials' aspirations is their deep desire for appreciation. Frequent, positive feedback is the best way to harness their energy and enthusiasm. But it's also important to show them how their contributions fit into the big picture. They want to know that their success and progress are directly related to their efforts.

- Recruiters looking to attract younger employees may want to stress the type of promotion opportunities that exist in their organization, regardless of age or tenure. Millennials are interested in promotions based on merit rather than on longevity.

4

Those *Other* Children of Boomers . . . Generation X

Parents often talk about the younger generation as if they didn't have anything to do with it.

—Haim Ginott

With all the attention being paid to the millions of Millennials now entering the workforce, we've somehow managed to lose a different generation. Before the Millennials, there was another group of Baby Boomer offspring that also made waves at work, albeit somewhat smaller waves.

Generation X, children who were born to Baby Boomers between the years of 1965 and 1979, began taking their places at work in the late 1980s and early 1990s. In many ways, this has become a forgotten generation, lost among all of the recent publicity surrounding Millennials.

To begin with, they are a smaller cohort than either Boomers or Millennials. Generation X has about half as many members as either of them, which have roughly the same amount. But what makes Gen Xers distinct from both Boomers and Millennials is that they grew up in a different era—with a different set of realities—and grew to adulthood with a different set of expectations.

While Gen Xers share a certain number of characteristics with Millennials and Boomers, they also have a unique perspective that has been overlooked by many. Any discussion about how the workforce is evolving in the early twenty-first century must include a look at the impact Generation X has had, and will have, on their employers. Over the course of the next few years, for example, members of Generation X will be assuming greater responsibility for managing Millennials, as they take the reins of authority from the hands of retiring Boomers.

What's in a Generation?

How do we define a generation? Are the members of a common generation defined solely by the years of their birth? Or are they better defined by the shared experiences of their formative years? Perhaps it is truly a combination of both.

When we look at the dividing lines between generations, we always encounter a certain amount of overlap. It's not uncommon for researchers to disagree over the set of birth dates that identify where the generational dividing line falls. This is less problematic with Baby Boomers, who were clearly the product of the years following World War II (as defined by the term "postwar baby boom").

The term "Echo Boomers," which has been assigned to the Millennials by some writers, would seem to be a neat distinction: simply the offspring of Baby Boomers. Yet, we find a greater distinction in looking at the first set of children born of the oldest set of Baby Boomers and giving them a separate identity from the youngest set, which we call Millennials.

Common sense suggests that it shouldn't be hard to identify who belongs to which generation. Simply looking at our own families tells us that the generations before us are our parents and our grandparents. The generations following us are, or will be, our children and grandchildren. No dates required! In reality, however, it's not that simple.

Going by the general age of consent in most societies, women begin to enter their childbearing years at age 18, which should be the beginning of the next generation. But when sociologists look at the average age at which women *actually* give birth to their first child, we discover a moving target.

Sociologists define a generation by calculating the average time between a mother's first offspring and her daughter's first offspring. By that calculation, a generation should average between 30 and 36 years in length. But recent changes in birthrates around the world have altered that calculation for the generations following the Baby Boomers.

To complicate matters further, birthrates vary throughout the world. For example, in the United States, the average age for first-time mothers is 25.2,[1] while in Great Britain, the average age is 27.4.[2] So, as the average age of childbirth begins to rise, it virtually guarantees that children born to the oldest members of the preceding generation may well have shared a very different set of experiences than the children born to the youngest members of the same generation. While Generation X and Millennials are both the descendents of the Baby Boom generation, there are going to be some very sharp contrasts between them, as well as a few similarities.

The Forgotten Generation

In recent years, there's been a bit of a backlash by members of Generation X against all of the attention their younger brothers and sisters—Millennials—have been receiving as they reached adulthood. In the book *X Saves The World: How Generation X Got the Shaft But Can Still Keep Everything From Sucking*, Gen X author Jeff Gordinier argues that the media created a false and negative impression of his cohort, even as they were tracking the exploits of Baby Boomers in minute detail and celebrating the rise of Millennials.

Far from accepting the slacker label pasted on his generation by a 1991 *TIME* magazine article, Gordinier explains (somewhat tongue-in-cheek) how, in many ways, Generation X has become the Rodney Dangerfield of generations. They simply "don't get no respect." According to the book, Generation X has given the world Google, YouTube, and Amazon, along with Gen X luminaries such as Quentin Tarantino and Jon Stewart.[3]

Although it was intended in fun, Gordinier's book also touched a nerve among many members of his generation. Similarly, a blog posted on *BusinessWeek*'s web site in 2008 generated a record number of responses from readers. The topic, "10 Reasons Gen Xers Are Unhappy at Work," apparently resonated with a great many people between the ages of 30 and 45 who shared similar frustrations with the blog's author, Tammy Erickson. Originally posted at *Harvard Business Online*, the article circulated extensively around the Internet, where frustrated Gen Xers agreed that they had been given the short end of the generational stick.[4]

Are the members of Generation X truly looked down on by Boomers? Does it even make sense that they would be similarly disparaged by Millennials? Perhaps. A certain amount of generational conflict seems to rear its head when young people begin to challenge (or at least annoy) their parents.

A well-respected thinker once said, "Children now love luxury; they have bad manners, contempt for authority; they show disrespect for elders and love chatter in place of exercise." It's instructive to remember that this oft-repeated quote was coined by the philosopher Socrates around 400 BC. Apparently some things never change!

But our frustration with a generation different than ours, whether that generation is above us or below us, also depends on which end of the generation gap we happen to be standing on. As songwriter Mike Rutherford of the rock group Genesis expressed in the song "Living Years": "Every generation blames the one before, and all of their frustrations come beating on your door."

If there is frustration growing among members of Generation X that they have not been taken seriously or given equal opportunities, it is at least partly a reflection of the fact that each generation is truly a product of its times. This seems to be especially so for Gen Xers, who grew up in a far more challenging environment than either the Boomers or the Millennials.

Before judging Generation X too harshly, we have to remember that they are truly a sandwich generation that has grown up in the shadow of the Baby Boom and Millennial generations. Gen Xers occupy a very special niche in the workforce and shouldn't be taken lightly. After all, who's to say they haven't changed the world?

They are only now beginning to come into their own. Born between 1965 and 1979, the members of Generation X are now reaching their early 30s to mid-40s. Within the organizational world, they are beginning to arrive among the ranks of middle managers, and in many cases are grooming for, if not actually entering, the top ranks of the corporate ladder.

Ironically, many members of Generation X will also be competing with those supremely confident rookies of the Millennial generation, who bring with them very high expectations for career success. In some cases, it's also very likely that new Millennial employees will mistakenly view their Gen X bosses as members of the Boomer generation.

And even though Millennials may well find themselves under the supervision of Gen Xers, the potential for conflict is very real. Anyone tasked with the challenge of managing the multigenerational workforce that includes members of all three generations will be very well advised to understand how Generation X differs from its predecessors and successors.

Defining the "X" Generation

So who *are* the members of this Generation X? They are the children of Baby Boomers, and they were born between 1965 and 1979. Their formative teenage years took place from around 1975 to 1985, with the bulk of them graduating college and entering the workforce from the late 1980s to the early 1990s.

By any reasonable assessment, these were dynamic years in history. It was a time bursting with amazing innovations and massive structural changes in the very fabric of our society. As the children of that period, Gen Xers as a population shared a very different set of childhood experiences than their parents and older siblings.

The first known instance of the term "Generation X" occurred in 1964 as part of a study conducted by a British women's magazine. The article's author, Jane Deverson, was writing about the habits of early 1960s teenagers, who were leading very different lives from their WWII-era parents. Deverson's research was rejected by the magazine, but she and coauthor Charles Hamblett later adapted the material for a book they titled *Generation X*. However, the writers were not attempting to define the Baby Boomer generation (which had already been so designated), but rather a subculture of that generation.[5]

A more direct source for the term "Generation X" is probably Canadian author Douglas Coupland. His 1991 novel, *Generation X: Tales for an Accelerated Culture,* tells the stories of three young adults in the late 1980s struggling to come to grips with meaningless jobs, unclear expectations, and hazy futures.[6] The novel was a slow starter but eventually developed a wide audience, and Coupland became a popular figure in the media as the voice of the new lost generation.

Slackers from the Grunge Generation

Whether intentional, Gen X unfortunately suffers from a somewhat negative reputation.

The common denominator for Boomer parents around the globe in the 1960s and 1970s was that the world had begun to truly recover from the political and economic disasters of the second world war. Even in countries that suffered most from World War II—Germany, Japan, and the Soviet Union—the 1970s represented a time of rising prosperity. Perhaps there is more than a little jealousy underlying the Baby Boomer parents' suspicion that their children had been spoiled and that they harbored unrealistic expectations.

Possibly the biggest culprit in slapping a negative label on Generation X was a widely read *TIME* magazine article published in 1990. The cover story, "Proceeding with Caution," took a hard look at the character of the younger generation, just then beginning to enter the workforce. Without apology, the authors painted a very dark portrait of how Generation X differed from their parents and how that would impact the workplace:

> By and large, the 18-to-29 group scornfully rejects the habits and values of the Baby Boomers, viewing that group as self-centered, fickle and impractical. While the Baby Boomers had a placid childhood in the 1950s, which helped inspire them to start their revolution, today's twenty-something generation grew up in a time of drugs, divorce and economic strain.
>
> They feel influenced and changed by the social problems they see as their inheritance: racial strife, homelessness, AIDS, fractured families and federal deficits.[7]

The negative attitudes and overall sense of cynicism described in the *TIME* article, as well as in other contemporary sources, soon led to Generation X being saddled with the label "Slacker generation." Another derogatory term applied to the generation, coined from the popularity of the Seattle-based band Nirvana, was the "Grunge generation." In either case, the meaning of the label is clear: The next generation was a group that neither expected much nor that much could be expected from.

To be sure, there were a number of social realities that uniquely influenced Generation X. For starters, the divorce rate in the United States doubled between 1963 and 1974, the formative years for most members of Generation X. In 1963, the divorce rate was 9.6 per 1,000 marriages, but by 1974, the rate was 19.3 divorces per 1,000 marriages.[8] This means that members of Generation X were the first "children of divorce." For many of them, growing up in a broken home meant high levels of family stress and economic instability.

At the same time, there was a corresponding rise in the number of women entering the workforce. This was partly the result of the rising birthrate. But it was also the result of increased opportunities for women, as well as increased awareness of the value of women's contributions to society. While this was a positive trend, it didn't necessarily bode well for children who were either being raised in single-parent households or in households where both parents were employed outside the home.

In this sense, Generation Xers became the first latchkey kids who were expected to fend for themselves upon arriving home after school. These conditions seem to create for many members of Generation X an overall feeling of being raised by absentee parents.

Also, for many Gen Xers, there was a very real sense that they might become the first generation to end up less well-off than their parents. The postwar economic boom, which took place in the United States from World War II until the mid-1960s, came to an abrupt end with the hyperinflation in the early 1970s and the global redistribution of wealth brought about by the second Arab Oil Embargo that lasted from October 1973 to March 1974. Through this time frame, there were many who saw America as becoming susceptible to diminished expectations.

By the time members of Generation X began graduating from college in the late 1980s, the economic climate they were entering was very different from the one their parents entered in the late 1960s and early 1970s. Between those decades, America had gone from being the undisputed economic powerhouse of the global economy to becoming just another competitor on the world stage for scarce resources and diminishing markets.

In 1980, Detroit automakers enjoyed a 50 percent share of the U.S. vehicle market. By the end of the decade, that share shrank to less than 30 percent, as Japanese and European carmakers made massive inroads into the buying public's affections. Likewise, the U.S. steel industry fell victim to stiffening competition in their markets by steelmakers from Europe and Asia.

Combine these massive shifts in the economy with the increased globalization of our markets, and you have an environment in which graduating Gen Xers had no confidence that they would be able to enjoy a steady career and a comfortable retirement. Faced with fewer job prospects, declining salaries, rising prices, and uncertain security, it's not surprising that many members of Generation X seemed bitter and cynical.

I Remember the '80s

It seems that no one ever objects to the use of the term "Baby Boomer" to describe the first generation following World War II. However, there are many people who seem to object to the term "Generation X" to describe the first cohort of Baby Boomer offspring. Among those objectors is Douglas Coupland, the author who originally coined the phrase. Although we may never replace the original term, some members of Generation X are suggesting that they be called the "Children of the '80s." And in some ways, that would be an appropriate phrase.

Several years ago, cable channel VH1 launched a nostalgia series entitled *I Love the 80s*. Not surprisingly, the viewership for this series included very large numbers of Gen Xers, who relished the chance to revisit their childhoods. In many ways, the decade of the 1980s was a cultural watershed. It is a period that saw major shifts in musical genres, the introduction of remarkable new technologies, global shifts in economic infrastructure, and evolutionary changes in popular culture, such as movies and television. But as radical as these years may seem to the casual observer, in many ways, the 1980s were a very special time for many people.

At the beginning of the decade, two musical trends challenged the reign of disco but also proved to be quite enduring. Rap music first developed a widespread following in the early years of the decade, and many early rap artists and music labels endure to this day. Likewise, the sound of punk groups, which rose in the early 1980s, returned to the simple rhythms of basic rock 'n' roll. Many punk artists and recordings remain popular to this day—in some cases, long after the groups quit performing.

The 1980s also witnessed a second "British invasion" in the musical world. Like the first British invasion of the early 1960s that brought us acts such as the Beatles, the Rolling Stones, the Who, and other legendary performers, the British invasion of the 1980s introduced the world to fresh new sounds. Acts such as Culture Club, the Eurhythmics, the Pet Shop Boys, Wham, Tears for Fears, and others invigorated the musical landscape for many Gen Xer youth.

In Hollywood, the development of computer-generated images (CGIs) heralded a new era in imagination and visual realism. Movies such as the *Star Wars* trilogy delivered dazzling new special effects that made it possible for filmmakers to explore previously unimaginable realms of fantasy. Many of the best movies from the 1980s introduced mind-blowing visual effects.

And we must not forget the revolutionary impact of personal computers throughout the decade of the 1980s. The introduction of the Apple II computer in the very late 1970s, along with the RadioShack TRS 80 and the Commodore 64, meant that the average household could now join the digital era. Along with video games, personal computers became the touchstone of the world's first truly digital generation, otherwise known as Generation X.

The 1980s also introduced exciting new communication technologies. The early products seemed huge and cumbersome in retrospect, but the first cell phones made their appearance in the 1980s. Even though they were expensive and bulky—with a very limited operating range—the idea of untethered phones captured the imagination of everyone.

But not every significant cultural event of the 1980s necessarily involved technology. In 1983, the popular movie *War Games*—starring a very young Matthew Broderick—suggested that a personal computer in the wrong hands could conceivably provoke a nuclear missile exchange between the United States and the Soviet Union. Ironically, the fall of the Berlin Wall in 1989 made the risk of that scenario suddenly seem very unlikely.

And what can be said about the fashion revolution of the 1980s? The fashion influences of the previous decade—the 1970s—ranged from the hippie-grunge-denim look that began the decade to the disco-glitter style that ended the decade. In contrast, the 1980s gave way to a wide variety of influences, including the *Miami Vice* look, the "Material Girl" style of Madonna, and torn sweatshirts (courtesy of the movie *Flashdance*). And who could ever forget legwarmers or parachute pants, or the new romantic London fashion, epitomized by pop groups like Duran Duran and Boy George?

But the newest fads of the 1980s didn't just challenge the ears or the eyes. The introduction of the Rubik's Cube also challenged the mind. To this day, millions of people remain frustrated in their fruitless quest to solve this three-dimensional game. Another 1980s fad that challenged the mind was a new board game called "Trivial Pursuit."

And speaking of games, one of the seminal events of the decade was the introduction of the Atari 2600 video game console. After starting with the simplest games—*Pong, Pac Man,* and *Space Invaders*—by the end of the decade, game players were enjoying *Super Mario Brothers, Legend of Zelda, Final Fantasy,* and similar entertainments.

Another electronic revolution that defined the decade of the 1980s was the introduction of home videotape systems. The early part of the decade witnessed a battle between two competing formats, VHS and Betamax (both invented by the Sony Corporation). Sony decided to back the technically-superior Betamax format and license VHS to other electronic firms. Ironically, the other electronic firms out-marketed Sony, and the VHS format ended up dominating the market, while Betamax eventually faded into oblivion.

But either way, the development of videotape recorders and players truly revolutionized how people experienced television and consumed movies. Throughout the 1980s, mom-and-pop video stores cropped up on nearly every corner, offering prerecorded movies and bags of popcorn to keep the average family busy during the weekend. Families also began compiling libraries of their favorite movies and forever changed the means by which Hollywood produced and marketed major motion pictures.

Even a casual review of some of the cultural touchdowns of the 1980s demonstrates why, for many people, it was a fun decade. Although there were significant cultural and economic undercurrents that threatened to change the fabric of society during the decade, there were plenty of new exciting things to do and see for a young generation growing up during that period.

A New Beat for a Young Generation

The 1980s introduced several new genres of music that have become enduring cultural fixtures for the members of Generation X. The early part of the decade saw a sharp contrast from the music of the 1970s, particularly disco music (which literally seemed to almost disappear overnight after January 1, 1980). As mentioned earlier, the 1980s saw the rise of new forms of music, including punk, pop, and rap.

The key artists that captured the imagination and loyalty of the music-listening public included the Police, U2, Michael Jackson, Prince, ABBA, Run DMC, the Beastie Boys, Public Enemy, and Madonna, among others.

Interestingly enough, music has a tendency to cross generational boundaries. At times, you will find an older generation reacting almost violently against their children's musical choices. This was so with swing music in the 1930s, rock 'n' roll in the 1950s, the Beatles in the 1960s, and rap music in the 1980s. In recent decades, however, the music of one generation often also appeals to a different generation. The music of the 1980s, for example, is very popular among Baby Boomers, who were young adults raising families during that decade. Likewise, much of the music of the Baby Boomer generation appeals to Millennials today. But one of the things that changed forever in the 1980s was the *technology* of music.

On August 1, 1981, a new cable channel called MTV was launched. MTV forever revolutionized how music was consumed and marketed. Now that modern music could be both viewed and listened to, radio top-40 playlists began to diminish in popularity. Videos enabled music publishers to garner the type of exposure they needed to sell lots of records without having to rely on massive promotional campaigns and the good graces of radio disc jockeys. In the words of the very first video MTV played that day, "Video killed the radio star."

The target audience for MTV was young listeners, primarily Generation X. However, a sufficient number of Baby Boomers listened to the music channel, so MTV created a second music network called Video Hits 1 (VH1). Ironically, MTV itself eventually shied away from playing music videos and began offering cultural programming, including reality TV shows.

But another change in the technology of music also affected Generation X. In the early 1980s, the Sony Corporation introduced the Walkman, a cassette-music player that featured a set of miniature earphones and a belt clip, enabling music lovers to take their music with them anywhere they chose. It was a big improvement over the enormous boom boxes of the 1970s, but it also meant that music became less of a shared experience.

Finally, we should mention another revolution in the music industry that occurred during the 1980s: the widespread introduction of compact disc (CD) players. CD players introduced digital music to the buying public, and as prices began to drop, music lovers began to give up their old vinyl records and cassette tapes in order to replace them with compact discs. This, of course, meant that everyone had to purchase the Beatles' "White album" all over again!

Perhaps no other period in history saw as many revolutionary changes, including new technologies, develop over such a short time span. And because these revolutionary changes occurred during the formative years of Generation X, it can safely be said that they were the very first digital generation in history. Just as the Millennial generation that followed, Gen Xers developed a very easy familiarity with technology and with change itself. These are skill sets that would serve both generations well when they began to enter the workplace.

However, many of the changes that occurred during the late 1970s and throughout the 1980s were primarily cultural phenomena.

The Era of the Teen Movie

The concept of a movie marketed exclusively to teenagers really came of age in the 1980s. The current success of movies like *High School Musical* demonstrates that this has been a very popular and lucrative strategy. However, the roots of the teen movie reach all the way back to the 1980s. It's instructive to look at the movies that appealed to teenagers during that decade, because it gives us a glimpse into the influences and the perceptions of the people we've come to call Generation X.

And if you're going to study the films of the 1980s, you must begin with the films of director John Hughes. Many of his movies were aimed at teenage audiences and in many ways came to characterize the youth of an entire generation. Films such as *Ferris Bueller's Day Off, The Breakfast Club,* and *Sixteen Candles* provided an almost sociological look at the formative years of Gen Xers.

In *Ferris Bueller's Day Off,* a perennially popular movie, high-school student Ferris Bueller manipulates the system (including changing his grades with a personal computer) to give himself a much-needed day off. In *Sixteen Candles,* we are treated to a look at the various cliques and subcultures that make up the population of a suburban high school, along with the snobbery and tensions that exist below the surface.

The Breakfast Club may well be the definitive 1980s teen movie. Set in a large suburban high school on a Saturday morning, a group of six teenagers serving detention share stories about the pressures and mistreatment they all suffer under the thumbs of their parents.

Although not strictly a 1980s teen movie, *St. Elmo's Fire* is the story of a group of seven recent college graduates in the mid-1980s who are struggling to establish themselves in careers while hoping to discover the meaning of happiness. It also stars a group of Generation X actors, whose joint appearance in several movies earned them the iconic nickname the "Brat Pack."

Other notable movies from the 1980s that were particularly popular among Gen Xers include *Heathers, Risky Business, War Games, The Karate Kid* (wax on . . . wax off), *Dirty Dancing,* and *Fast Times at Ridgemont High.*

The common thread all of these movies share is not only were they immensely popular with Generation X, but also, in some way, each of these movies tells us something about what it was like to grow up in that period. Despite relative affluence and the presence of a great deal of new technology, you can see that Gen Xers may have suffered from the anxiety of high expectations and the absence of parents, most of whom were either disengaged or preoccupied.

We should also note here that these are obviously all distinctively American films. Although a great many outstanding films were produced around the world during the 1980s, it seems safe to point out that it was primarily American filmmakers who produced the genre we call teen movies. One exception is the animated film *Akira* that was produced in Japan in 1988. Although the film is a postapocalyptic science-fiction tale, the principal characters are teenagers who struggle with the same sense of disaffection and alienation one can see in American teen movies from the same period. Not surprisingly, *Akira* has also been very popular with members of Generation X, as well as among Millennials.

A Generation Shaped by Television

Movies were not the only cultural phenomenon to influence Gen Xers during their formative years. It goes without saying that television, particularly in America, had a huge impact on many of the perceptions and sensibilities of Generation X. Among the changes that occurred in the landscape of television was the advent of the Cable News Network (CNN), the first channel to deliver news 24-7.

In fact, the number of available television channels expanded dramatically during the decade of the 1980s. Whereas the Baby Boomers essentially grew up with four channels, their children had a cornucopia of hundreds of channels from which to select. However, some of the most influential television shows from that era were originally broadcast on the Big Three networks.

The long-running series M*A*S*H and another shorter-lived series called China Beach gave members of Generation X a very different perspective on war—essentially, the message that war is bad.

One of the most popular television shows of the 1980s, Miami Vice, was the first show to mix drama with popular music. The show's creator, NBC president Brandon Tartikoff, described the show as "MTV cops." Landmark comedy series the Cosby Show significantly broke racial barriers and became the top-rated network television show for five years running. It was also the harbinger of the diversity movement.

Another comedy, Family Ties, pitted a pair of liberal Baby Boomer parents against their conservative Generation X children. That, too, may have been a harbinger of things to come. The 1980s also featured shows, such as St. Elsewhere and Hill Street Blues, that brought a nonidealized gritty sense of reality to network television. Reality on TV also got a boost when the reality TV shows, Real People and That's Incredible, were produced in the 1980s. And Baby Boomers weren't underrepresented during the 1980s, either. The comedy series The Wonder Years taught Gen Xers what it was like to grow up during their Baby Boomer parents' childhoods.

Making History in the 1980s

Besides the cultural technological changes in society that marked the decade of the 1980s, we also have to look at the major events that tended to shape the worldview of Generation X while growing up during those years. Even a small sampling of the major news stories of the period demonstrates what a history-making era the decade truly was:

- In the early 1980s, Japanese carmakers Honda, Toyota, Mazda, and Nissan really began to make serious inroads into the domestic share of the automobile market, which had long been dominated by General Motors, Ford, Chrysler, and American Motors (which did not survive the decade).
- In 1980, the United States boycotted the Moscow Olympics in protest over the Soviet Union's invasion of Afghanistan. Four years later, Eastern Bloc athletes boycotted the 1984 Los Angeles Olympics in retaliation. The Goodwill Games were launched in an attempt to reconcile the feuding parties and take politics out of world athletics.
- In 1980, the Beatles founder John Lennon was assassinated outside his New York apartment.
- In 1981, Prince Charles of Great Britain married Diana Spencer in ceremonies that were viewed by hundreds of millions of people around the world.
- The Reagan era came to define politics from 1980 to 1988. During that time, Reagan fired unionized air-traffic controllers who were on strike, greatly expanded the federal budget, negotiated new antimissile treaties with the Soviets, and presided over the largest deregulation of business in American history.
- The early 1980s saw rise of the deadly new AIDS virus. The disease soon became a worldwide crisis.
- The year 1983 saw the launch of the space shuttle enterprise and the first American woman go into space (Sally Ride).
- An accidental gas leak at a Union Carbide facility in Bhopal, India, released toxic gas that resulted in the deaths of more than 3,000 residents in 1984.
- A massive famine in the African country of Ethiopia led to the Live Aid global fund-raising concerts in 1985.

- In January 1986, the space shuttle Challenger exploded shortly after its launch, killing all seven crew members, including high-school teacher Christa McAuliffe.
- The world watched in trepidation during the spring of 1986, as a Soviet nuclear reactor in the town of Chernobyl failed, resulting in a massive meltdown.
- In 1987, the American economy took another hit following the largest stock market crash since the Great Depression.
- The Berlin Wall, a landmark of the Cold War era, came crashing down in 1989 after a crumbling Soviet Union withdrew its troops from eastern Germany.
- One of the largest ecological disasters in history took place in 1989, when the oil tanker Exxon Valdez ran aground in Alaska's Prince William Sound.
- The cause of democracy in Communist China was dealt a serious setback when the Chinese government implemented a brutal crackdown on prodemocracy demonstrators occupying Beijing's Tiananmen Square in 1989.

Clearly, the course of world history during the 1980s proved to Generation X that neither security nor safety could be taken for granted, and that institutions once thought impregnable could be brought down, sometimes in ruin.

The Sandwich Generation

Generation X has been referred to by many different names in recent years. One term that seems particularly appropriate is the "Sandwich generation." While this term has also been applied to Baby Boomers who find themselves sandwiched between raising young children on the one hand and caring for elderly parents on the other, the term may also be applicable to Generation X for very different reasons.

Generation X has, in fact, been sandwiched between their dominating Baby Boomer parents on one hand and the supremely confident Millennials on the other hand. Not only are those two generational cohorts larger than the Generation X cohort, but members of both the Boomer and Millennial generations are influential movers and shakers. Combined, they can be a tough act to follow, as well as to precede.

Gen Xers frequently express frustration with limited job opportunities and slow career progress, brought about by increasingly flat organizations and tough economic conditions. And just as they are reaching positions of authority, Gen Xers are encountering a new level of economic distress that threatens to deny them their rewards for keeping their noses to the grindstone and paying their dues. It's understandable that some may even feel a little threatened by the so-called unlimited potential of Gen Yers, who are now beginning to compete with them for the same future.

There may always be a lingering fear of organizational downsizing and layoffs in the back of Gen Xers' minds. However, as they reach their mid-30s and early 40s, the members of Generation X are also beginning to feel the pinch of family pressures. So, it's only natural that many are resentful that they may be stuck in dead-end positions at the very time in life when their family needs are beginning to rise. Put this all together, and it's a recipe for the sandwich generation that many Gen Xers are not going to find easy to swallow.

Gen Xers versus Millennials

As the offspring of the Baby Boom generation find themselves in growing contact with each other within an organization, they will both be able to take the measure of the other. When they do, they will perhaps find that they have more in common with each other than expected. But without question, there are also clear distinctions in how members of each generation communicate, solve problems, perceive, think, and react. The following are just a few of the differences that distinguish members of each generation:

- Gen Xers tend to take a pragmatic approach to solving problems, whereas Millennials tend to approach problems with a strong sense of self-confidence in their ability to find an answer.

- The latchkey children, Generation X, developed a very strong sense of self-reliance, having done a lot of things on their own. Millennials, on the other hand, have grown up with "helicopter" parents, upon whom they have relied for guidance at all major turning points.

- Generation X has a reputation for distrusting the rules and taking a skeptical approach to policy. Millennials, on the other hand, have a reputation for rewriting the rules they don't like. This should prove interesting in resolving workplace issues.

- Again, although Generation X is indeed technology oriented, they have sometimes been slow to adopt the newest technologies. Gen Yers weren't merely exposed to technology growing up—they were literally immersed in it and may prove to be quicker in adopting the latest and greatest gee-whiz technologies.

- Members of Generation X are noted for forming strong relationships and deep friendships. Millennials have demonstrated very strong bonds of friendship; however, they tend to define friendship in much looser and less relationship-intensive terms. For example, the friends that Millennials collect on the Internet site Facebook are often people with whom they have no real relationship, but who they still consider friends.

- If you want a job done right, the members of Generation X would say do it yourself. In contrast, Millennials would say do it with a team.

- Gen Xers may well be the original multitaskers, and they are very skilled at handling multiple priorities. However, Millennials also multitask and have earned a reputation as hyper-multitaskers.

As the members of each generation gain greater exposure to members of the other generation, both groups will find common cause and many similarities to celebrate. If we look at them as teammates, you see two groups who bring to their organization a very strong set of skills and a mutual desire to achieve great things. Far from being competitive, Gen Xers and Millennials could well become powerful allies and outstanding teammates.

Motivating Gen Xers

If we were to advise managers who were charged with the task of integrating a work team composed of both Generation X and Millennials, we would tell them to build a climate of mutual trust, risk taking, and high expectations. The type of workplace that motivates the members of any generation to strive for the best is a workplace that will appeal to all generations and not just one type of employee. If you do find yourself managing members of Generation X or Millennials, you need to create a climate that is built upon the following strategies:

- **Provide fulfilling work and challenging assignments.** Never forget that the work itself should be the primary motivating factor, no matter who your employees are. This includes making sure that employees understand the meaning of the work and recognize the importance of their efforts. Once employees feel as though their efforts count—as though they make a difference—then individual differences in communication or problem-solving style will not become significant barriers to accomplishment.
- **Build individual relationships.** In order to create a true team, you have to teach your employees to develop a genuine sense of appreciation for each other's skills, strengths, and weaknesses. An effective team consists of people who are

willing to take advantage of differences in skills and perceptions in order to make the team's efforts stronger.

- **Recognize individual accomplishment.** One of the fundamental differences between Gen Xers and Millennials is their degree of patience with teamwork. Millennials have been taught to value team efforts, while Gen Xers have grown up somewhat skeptical of functioning within a group. The way to appeal to both of those sensibilities is to make sure that you provide plenty of recognition for the individual accomplishments of people, either within a team or working on their own.

- **Provide plenty of feedback.** Whether employees come from the Millennial generation or Generation X, you can be sure that they will respond well to lots of positive reinforcement and structured feedback. Millennials actually crave lots of feedback, and Generation X has learned to be comfortable with it. If feedback is the "breakfast of champions," you can be sure that you will be managing a stable of thoroughbreds by making regular, constructive feedback part of your employees' daily diet.

Looking at the big picture, it would be impossible to manage a productive multigenerational workforce if you were not able to understand and address the individual needs and concerns of every generation within your workplace. That having been said, many of the differences and conflicts between the generations are more perception than reality, as long as you understand that you have to manage people from these generational groups as individuals and not as stereotypes.

By providing these perspectives on the similarities and differences between Generation X, Baby Boomers, and Millennials, we hope you will gain greater insights into the genuine strengths and the special gifts of each generation. A truly totally harmonious workforce may really be nothing more than a pipe dream. But information is power, and each of the generations within your team are capable of contributing the creativity and drive your organization needs to succeed, perhaps even beyond its wildest dreams.

Keys to Chapter 4

- Members of Generation X are the children of Baby Boomers, and they were born between 1965 and 1979. Their formative teenage years took place from around 1975 to 1985, with the bulk of them graduating college and entering the workforce from the late 1980s to the early 1990s.

- The term "Generation X" originated with Canadian author Douglas Coupland's 1991 novel *Generation X: Tales for an Accelerated Culture.*

- Baby Boomers seem to express a negative view of Gen Xers. A widely read *TIME* magazine article published in 1990 painted a very dark portrait of how Generation X differed from their parents and how that would impact the workplace.

- With a high divorce rate in the late 1960s and 1970s, Generation Xers were the first "children of divorce."

- Generation X became the first latchkey kids who were expected to fend for themselves upon arriving home after school.

- The decade of the 1980s was a cultural watershed that saw major shifts in musical genres, the introduction of remarkable new technologies, global shifts in economic infrastructure, and evolutionary changes in popular culture, such as movies and television.

- Generation Xers have suffered from a more negative view of their generation, as compared to those before and after them.

- Generation X can be called the very first digital generation in history. Just as the Millennial generation that followed, Gen Xers developed a very easy familiarity with technology and with change itself.

- The course of world history and the major events that occurred during the 1980s proved to Generation X that neither security nor safety could be taken for granted, and that institutions once thought impregnable could be brought down, sometimes in ruin.

- There may always be a lingering fear of organizational downsizing and layoffs in the back of Gen Xers' minds. However, as they reach their mid-30s and early 40s, the members of Generation X are also beginning to feel the pinch of family pressures.

- Managers charged with the task of integrating a work team composed of both Generation X and Millennial employees should build a climate of mutual trust, risk taking, and high expectations. The type of workplace that motivates the members of any generation to strive for the best is a workplace that will appeal to all generations and not just one type of employee.

5

Creating a Millennial-Friendly Culture

A leader may chart the way . . . [but] many leaders and many peoples must do the building.

—Eleanor Roosevelt

No matter how cool your company may appear to Millennial job candidates, once you have them on board, it's imperative that you also provide a cool work environment. Salary, perks, and other things that may originally have drawn them to your organization aren't going to keep them loyal if they find the work to be drudgery and their bosses to be slugs.

In fact, Millennials place a high priority on finding a job that takes advantage of their talents and maintains their interest level. Perks alone won't provide that type of opportunity. You have to make sure that your managers are offering plenty of feedback and the right kind of structure that energizes Millennials and makes them feel appreciated.

This requires a well-thought-out system of on-the-job training, leadership development, and team building. It's a matter of making sure your company's best practices incorporate effective leadership, including how you develop the weakest and strongest of your recruits. There are a number of strategies to accomplish this.

Make Sure You Tag the Keepers

In an ideal world, every employee would be brimming with competence and potential. Sadly, that's not the actual world. To put it bluntly, every group of recent recruits is going to be filled with its share of winners and losers. Some will manage to learn quickly, adapt easily, and rise to the surface. Then there are going to be those who remain clueless, slow to adapt, and stuck in the middle. At some point, you'll have to make a choice between promising employees and those with less ability.

That's why it's good to identify the people you want to keep. It may not always be the people that you know directly. You may have seen and observed their performance, or you may have simply heard of them in other departments. Either way, you want to make sure that these promising employees get tagged as keepers—people you simply don't want to lose.

The first step is to make sure you let them know that you consider them to be keepers. Leaving them in the dark about the fact that you consider them to be promising does nothing for their self-esteem. And it may actually end up sending the message that you don't care about them. "It meant a lot to me when my boss told me how much I was valued," stated one Millennial. "Some days I didn't even think she noticed me, let alone what I was doing. I was actually considering leaving the company before she told me how much she appreciated me."

Another Millennial shares this story:

> I had just thought about leaving, because for the first time, I was feeling like I was sort of going nowhere. My boss had been ill and off for some time over the past six months, and no one paid very much attention to me. It seemed to come out of nowhere that my boss let me know that she didn't want to lose me and mentioned several projects of mine that had really impressed her. I stayed and was promoted two months later.

So, if you do care about them and have high expectations for their future, let them know. Millennials like to feel appreciated and valued. They need to know that they are making an honest-to-goodness contribution to your organization. If they feel the work they are doing does not matter, they'll lose enthusiasm and become disengaged.

But let's be honest. Most jobs carry their share of monotony and boring routine. Reports, meetings, grunt work, and endless details can be a drag. Although it's impossible to avoid this part of work completely, it's in any company's best interest to minimize it, particularly in the case of Millennials.

One way to do that is to challenge your Millennials to take on more, or different, responsibilities. Toss them a challenge. Ask them to pick up the slack on an important goal or to undertake an exciting new project. If you scratch below the surface, you'll find that a significant number of Millennials had a great deal of varied responsibilities while still in secondary school, such as jobs, band, sports clubs, and volunteer work. These things brought them recognition and attention, which they still crave at work. Assigning younger employees to special projects is a very effective way of confirming their value to the organization and reinforcing their future potential.

But make sure you do it right. The special projects that you assign can't be mere busywork. The goals must be made clear, and the importance of the project to the future of your organization needs to be highlighted. And it doesn't hurt to let them know that upper management is keeping an eye on the project.

Another way to engage the Millennials is to cross-train them for other jobs throughout the organization. Some of the most innovative organizational onboarding programs place new recruits into a variety of jobs for a limited period of time before their final position in the company is determined. Millennials appreciate that type of broad exposure.

It's also critical to discuss career advancement. As organizations have become flatter over the past few decades, it's become harder to show clear-cut career paths. This is especially problematic for your fast-track employees. You don't want them to get the notion that the only way they can advance more quickly is by job-hopping from your company to another one.

Two Millennial, who tried faithfully to hang on for a promotion that never materialized, revealed:

> I worked like crazy to get ahead—sixty- or seventy-hour work weeks. I was told upon hire it would take one year to get promoted. After three years and hearing it would take five, I left for a commission job and a new career.
>
> I left after losing a promotion to an outside hire because I had one-and-a-half years experience and he had the two years required in the job posting. It wasn't bad enough that he got the job, but then I was expected to train him. As soon as I found a new job I left.

One way to gain their longer-term commitment is to make sure they have continual learning and development opportunities. These might take the form of company workshops, assessment centers, outside training, or tuition reimbursement. The sooner you start, the better, because Millennials are not noted for their patience, and many need development, as described in Chapter 7.

Finally, remember that the most important role your keepers may play in your organization is to be the first group of Millennials to replace the retiring Baby Boomer generation. Take a close look at your organization's profile to determine how many key positions you will have to replace between now and 2014 (and beyond). You will want the best people available to fill those roles. You may as well begin grooming them now.

How Do You Spot the Others?

It would truly be great if every new employee we recruited turned out to be a bona fide winner, but we have to face reality. Not all new employees cut it, and the sooner you identify and act on the underperforming people, the better off your organization is going to be. Few managers like to sit down to tell someone that he or she isn't performing up to standard, but you have to learn to spot problem employees quickly and take action. If you ignore employee performance problems, you risk winding up with a barrel of bad apples and hands full of productivity and discipline problems.

Why are bad apple employees such a problem? Make sure you don't fall into these common pitfalls:

1. *Bad Apples can spread through an organization like a virus.*

Some companies tolerate managers passing bad apples from department to department. Rather than try to bring their bad apple's behavior to an end, many managers choose to simply move the employee on to another department. By the time they get to you, they've been with the company for so long that it seems impossible to fire them. You're tempted to follow the lead of your predecessors and simply shuffle your bad apples along to the next team—but all that does is move around the misery. Millennials, like other generations, don't want to pull someone else's weight—especially a low performer.

Take it from one Millennial's experience: "I started the job a day after the office manager was fired. Can you believe she had been there 17 years, moving from department to department until someone had the courage to let her go? Whatever . . ."

2. *Coworkers become frustrated and angry.*

Some managers expect team members to deal with the bad apple, but people have a great deal of difficulty giving feedback to their peers. Millennials are not inclined toward negative feedback, anyway. They'll almost always push the problem back to managers rather than confront the employee directly. At worst, team members become sullen and resentful that poor performance is being tolerated, and overall performance can suffer.

Consider a department manager's dilemma:

I was tired of getting copied on e-mails evidencing poor performance of the e-mailer's coworker. The e-mailer kept asking me to
deal with this poor performer whose mistakes were not evident
to me; however, she did not want to be involved. I finally got them
in a room together and insisted that the e-mailer explain how the
poor performer was also negatively impacting her work. I docu-
mented the discussion and continued to coach the women and
watch over the situation.

3. *Bad apples can distract you from managing good performance.*

Rather than model and recognize the behavior they want,
expect, and demand, managers often focus too much attention
on poor behavior, as in the squeaky wheel gets the oil. There's
just something in human nature that allows the bad to outweigh
the good, but you can't miss the opportunity to give high performers positive feedback. And Millennials thrive on positive
feedback.

"You know, my reward for good work has been more work,
and I'm tired of it!" said one Millennial. "I have a coworker who
takes all of my boss's time because his work is so bad. Just let me
know once in a while that I'm valuable. Say it to me or give
me a $300 reward at our next meeting."

4. *The threat of repercussions can cause management paralysis.*

Some managers are so afraid to fire bad apples for fear of
legal retribution that they end up accepting mediocrity. What
message is that sending to your younger Millennial hires? Bad
apples, by definition, are troublemakers, and it stands to reason
that people who cause problems working inside a company
are likely to also cause problems on their way out the door. If
you're like many managers, you may fear that if you fire your bad
apples—or even confront or discipline them—they'll threaten

to file suit for discrimination or harassment or any other reason they think will work.

A Boomer, admitting that she left a termination up to her successor, says:

> I'm embarrassed to tell you that I didn't take a step that I should have before I left my employer for another job. I had coached and disciplined a young employee whose performance was, from the start, marginal. He was a good person, seemed to try hard, but never really cut it. I guess I just didn't want to confront the fact that I couldn't get him to a better level of performance. Maybe I just didn't want to admit that I made a bad hire.

5. *Firing employees, no matter how bad their behavior or performance, isn't easy.*

If bad apples refuse to change their behavior, the time will come when you must let them go. Unfortunately, firing people is such an unpleasant experience that most managers will put it off for as long as possible. They risk losing the respect that they need from all employees, especially Millennials they want to keep.

Take it from one Millennial who said, "It drives me nuts to see some of my coworkers 'coasting' at work, just getting by. My boss just pretends it's okay. I don't know why it's tolerated, unless my boss just wants to put in time also."

Obviously, you have to have well-structured systems in place in your organization to help unproductive employees either improve their performance or to help them as they exit the company. Don't hold on to them needlessly, and don't accept marginal performance.

When it comes to correction and discipline, no employee likes to be on the receiving end of one of those dreaded discussions. And when it comes to Millennials, they are no different than their predecessors. They don't like to be told that they're not performing. But they really do like and seek out feedback.

So long as your methods for providing feedback are structured and objective—preferably with concrete measures—you may be surprised at how well these employees respond. But also remember that if Millennial employees don't see a future with your organization, they are probably also more likely to solve your problem by moving on.

However, bear in mind that there is a very critical reason your organization cannot afford to put up with mediocre employee performance: The kind of atmosphere that supports mediocrity would be a major turn off to your better-performing Millennials. It's like we always used to say, "One bad apple spoils the barrel!" So, take action to weed out those employees who are bringing your overall productivity down and demotivating the good performers.

Making Diversity Count

Perhaps no other generation in history has been so immersed in the diversity that exists within the global marketplace as Millennials have. Millennials have grown up living the reality that individual differences contribute to team synergy and innovation. They have learned to celebrate and embrace diversity, and they expect that same type of culture to exist in the organizations they join. We have personally witnessed numerous Millennial interns in our business that have changed universities to transfer to more diverse ones. Millennials also look for global awareness in the workplace as one criterion in selecting an employer.

For example, one large manufacturing organization built discussions about differences directly into its very elaborate new employee onboarding program. In one of their presentations, employees with special needs were invited to meet with new recruits to discuss how their needs were integrated into the organization and to explain the particular challenges they encountered every day. Not only was this discussion good for team building, inclusion, and awareness, but it also built relationships among people who may have been slow to connect otherwise.

And remember that in an increasingly global marketplace, the awareness of different cultures is a critical component in successfully doing business. The more sensitive your new employees are to these differences, the more effective they will be at recognizing and overcoming certain obstacles that diversity may cause.

Make sure to avoid these five biggest traps when leading a diverse team:

1. *Not valuing differences*

When leaders see differences as an advantage, they seek diversity in their teams and work hard to get the different perspectives and opinions on the table. What are you doing to bring in the fresh perspective of youth? Are younger members of your team part of problem-solving sessions? Are they invited to provide input to strategy and operational plans?

2. *Failure to create an inclusive environment*

You need to encourage the involvement of all team members, who in turn need to feel comfortable about offering suggestions and challenging ideas or practices. Help Millennials present their ideas to the rest of the team. They may have the greatest suggestions but lack the experience of influencing others. You demonstrate inclusion by being open to new ideas, listening to different perspectives, and encouraging creative problem solving.

3. *Stereotyping*

Avoid associating any behaviors, talents, or lack of abilities with any particular group. For instance, any leader who assumes that all women are emotional, all Millennials are immature, or all

Asians are excellent in math is guilty of prejudice and does not acknowledge the uniqueness of each individual.

4. *Not modeling the expected behaviors*

Effective leaders demonstrate the behaviors they want from others. When you show respect for differences, develop trust in your team, and promote the value of differences, you set the standard for how others should behave. Watch for and confront any behaviors that are less than accepting or derogatory to any team members. You should clearly communicate that disrespect for others will not be tolerated.

5. *Failure to coach*

You need to make expectations clear to all employees and coach them individually toward higher levels of performance and growth. Besides the individual coaching, help your teams with conflicts that may arise, such as friction between the generations. And also encourage team members to coach others.

Don't assume that your Millennial employees will have a huge advantage over their Boomer or Mature predecessors in embracing differences. The Boomers are also particularly attuned to the issue, since they were the ones who marched for civil rights and equal rights for women, along with many other social causes.

Your organization's approach to managing differences could send a powerful message to younger workers that all employees are valued and respected for their contributions. Such a message can turn out to be the very foundation on which to build a culture.

Release the Shackles

We all know why new ideas wither on the vine and die in most organizations. It's because "we've never done it that way around here."

Or because "we tried that once and it didn't work," or "that would never work around here." Instead, a constant mantra for leaders who want to continue to create innovation should be, "What if?" It opens up creative thinking, giving employees the freedom to explore a multitude of options.

If you are trying to create an environment that is engaging and exciting for Millennial workers, you're going to have to ask yourself whether your work culture truly supports fresh ideas and new thinking. Most workplace cultures don't! In KEYGroup's 2006 survey, only 20 percent of the 1,727 respondents considered their company to be innovative. Employee teams often become much too caught up in the implicit rules, procedures, and customs of the daily routine in their department. If this is the type of culture your organization possesses, it may well prove to be poison to younger employees.

Most Millennials are simply looking for a chance to contribute. They have a high opinion of their abilities, and they expect to be heard. When they run into entrenched procedures and static rules, they very quickly become frustrated and lose their motivation. It's critical for you to take a look at your workplace environment ahead of recruiting younger employees. You need to determine whether the rules—written or unspoken—need to be reexamined, changed, or enforced as they are. Consider the difficulty that the Boomers are causing in the following example.

As one Millennial said:

My firm recruits from the best colleges and only hires entry-level designers that have been trained on state-of-the-art technology and software. The Boomer-aged employees at our firm are not required to learn this new technology or are reluctant to use it. My number one complaint in working for Boomer bosses is their lack of knowledge in new technology. Since our firm revolves around technology, some older employees are, in a sense, costing the firm money by not knowing architectural software. Sketches need to be done by hand and then given to a younger, more tech-savvy worker to be put into a software format. We are adding another step to the design process. Time is money in the architectural field.

Flexibility is another critical factor when you're dealing with Millennial employees. It's true they may lack experience or a certain kind of street smarts. However, they also bring a pair of fresh eyes and an untainted mind. They could well discover some new ways to do things that are ultimately more productive and successful.

As the leader, you need to set the standard for maintaining an open mind. Do you have work rules that are outdated? Are there characteristics of your culture that preclude fresh thinking? Are you and your employees open to suggestion, or are you more set in your ways? If so, you can count on the Millennials to shake things up.

A frustrated Millennial shared:

> From a technology perspective, my company is rather stifling. Restricted Internet access is a major concern that causes incredible inefficiencies. The inability to access research-related web sites often forces employees to take their work home. Having capacity restrictions on the e-mail system is another troubling flaw. At one point, more than half of my department was unable to send e-mail due to capacity restrictions. These restrictions take days to rectify, only to reoccur again after the next limit is exceeded.

This is a generation that somehow has developed the philosophy that it's better to ask for forgiveness than for permission. They may have learned this lesson from their Boomer parents, or it simply may come with that broad sense of entitlement Millennials seem to possess. It's not unusual for Millennials to challenge age-old traditional practices.

Frankly, if you can't satisfactorily explain your company rules and traditions, it's time for a change! And if you don't see the truth of that, your Millennial recruits will be very quick to tell you.

One Millennial was "corrected" for taking a longer lunch. He challenged the correction by telling his boss that he had not taken lunch on the previous two days and had informed his coworker that he would be 30 minutes longer. His boss said that he should have asked his permission.

When you begin to bring Millennial employees into your workforce, you could well encounter a number of conflicts that could cause friction within your work team. The Millennials bring with them a very different sense of appropriate dress, for example, and they could well make casual Fridays look like a day at the beach.

Millennials also have very strong opinions about ergonomic workspaces, start and stop times, and the availability of free time. These attitudes could be a turnoff to existing employees—and yes, it is usually incumbent upon new employees to adapt themselves to the existing staff. But if you turn a blind eye to the feedback you may be getting from Millennials, you may miss a chance to create a more dynamic environment. You could create a work climate that employees of all generations could well find exhilarating!

Because I Said So!

In the past, leaders in most organizations fell back on the authority that came with tenure and titles. People who'd served in the job longest, people who came up through the ranks—often slowly but steadily—and people who had achieved rank were the ones who called the shots. Many Mature and Boomer leaders behaved in a "do as I say, not as I do" manner. Employees were expected to automatically give loyalty and compliance to these managers, which won't fly with the Millennials, particularly if the boss lacks competence.

For example, the *Dilbert* cartoon, created by Scott Adams, consistently mocks what he calls "pointy-haired" bosses. They are typically people with little real authority who go out of their way to interfere with the efforts of competent employees below them.

Even on television and in the movies, the image of incompetent leaders crops up as a classic archetype. Take the comedy series *The Office* as a current example. Apparently, it's a great comedic element

Some ideas for leaders include:

- Be careful not to ask employees to do something you wouldn't do.

- Be circumspect about behaving the way you expect others to behave.

- Avoid making negative comments behind people's backs.

- Encourage and model work-life balance.

- Cultivate teamwork by pitching in, even if it's not part of your normal responsibilities.

to have incapable people in charge. In real life, however, it's a recipe for disaster.

The lesson is that those who lead Millennial employees need to establish respect through what they do, because it won't come due to their titles.

Think about "Brand You"

It pays for a leader to think about his or her reputation or image. You need to find ways to inspire your followers. Some leaders do it by example. Some leaders do it by creating a vivid vision. Others do it by administering a well-defined structure or by building a culture of excellence.

Think about what you hope to be known for as a leader. Do you expect to be seen as a stickler for the rules or as more relaxed about your expectations? Will your employees see you as a good communicator or as someone who is difficult to read? Obviously, your reputation will rise and fall with the accomplishments of your team. However, how you are viewed externally within your organization may be a far cry from how you are viewed within your department.

To create "Brand You" as a leader, reflect on the following questions, and craft your vision, values, and goals based on:

1. What legacy do I want to leave?

2. How do I want to be viewed by internal and external customers?

3. What core values do I espouse and live by, and how will I demonstrate them?

4. What mantra do I expect myself and others to live by?

5. What is my dream for what I'd like to accomplish with my team?

6. What specific goals will get us there?

More often than you can imagine, leaders prefer to cultivate a reputation as being demanding and austere rather than being friendly and accessible. Unfortunately, the former tends to be old-school thinking. It's reminiscent of the "my way or the highway "attitude. It's the signature of a leader who expects to be obeyed unquestioningly, whether that leader is actually right—or even competent.

As discussed previously, Millennials are more inclined to respect leaders who practice what they preach. These types of leaders are not afraid to get in the trenches and get their hands dirty. To be an effective leader, especially in a multigenerational environment, one must give serious consideration to the values that drive his or her behavior and guide the conduct of his or her employees. Paying attention to how you set expectations among your team members and following through on goals and assignments are critical components to functioning in an effective way.

As an example, in one of our client companies, a new vice president was brought in to turn around a highly visible failing unit. The first thing she did—day one of the job—was hold a full team meeting to discuss her vision, values, and expectations and to address key questions and challenges posed by her team. She wanted to be branded as a visionary and approachable leader, starting with the first touch in the organization.

Try Not to Make Work, "Work"

Where did any of us ever get the idea that the concept of work is completely independent from the concept of play? Maybe it goes back to our early school years, when we were ushered back in from the playground so we could take out a math book and "get down to work." It's common for work and leisure to be seen as two separate pursuits. However, nowadays, we know better.

Work doesn't have to be all drudgery, and the end of the work shift doesn't need to be the highlight of most workers' days! How many times have we wandered through an office in the morning, only to be struck by the number of zombies that show up for work? After all, if your employees start the day dispirited and filled with bored resignation, how much is getting accomplished by the end of that day, or by the end of the week?

But leaders today are beginning to question the old assumptions. Why should work not be as challenging and fun as a video game? Why can there not be enthusiasm and joy in the workplace? Is it not possible to tap the natural energy that humans bring to any fun pursuit?

If you fall into the former camp—the work is drudgery camp— you may be in for quite a shock when the Millennial generation begins to enter your workplace. They expect work to be challenging and fun. They expect success to be rewarded. They expect their talents to be utilized and recognized. And if work doesn't meet these expectations, your Millennial employees won't be with you for very long, or they will be there but not be as productive as they could be.

Be zany—add fun to the workplace. Consider some of these zany ideas that we have observed in our client companies:

- Every project has a movie brand, and each team member is cast in one of the lead supporting roles. Teams score cards are displayed in movie storyboard fashion.
- A child's pink toy pony is used to "catch someone doing something right," given to an employee through video fanfare and posted on the company's TV for that three-week period.
- A CEO-endorsed "Whiner Award," not given very frequently, is provided to any employee who complains about something and doesn't provide a possible solution or recommendation for improvement.
- A tiny ceramic chocolate-chip cookie is given to an employee by a supervisor or coworker to acknowledge an outstanding contribution. Why chocolate chip? It was the favorite cookie of the CEO. Once an employee accumulates a dozen, he or she gets a dozen homemade ones baked by the CEO.
- A cowbell rings in the foyer when a new account is brought in.
- A pool table and football game was added to the expanded employee break room.
- Each department is responsible no more than one time per year to orchestrate a themed parade, costumes and all. One never knows when the parade might happen.
- Employees informed of a two-hour meeting were surprised to find out that they were going bowling.
- A local theater was rented to introduce a new product, and for those who could stay, a free movie was available.
- Brainstorming sessions include toys, props, musical instruments, costumes, and hats to foster creativity.
- The senior level and midmanagement team serves lunch.
- Without warning, a team of masseuses shows up to give shoulder rubs to employees.

- People come into work to find a packet of 25 stars to be distributed to those who have been nice to them.
- A CEO is rewarded with one more Pez dispenser each time something good happens.
- An employee who takes charge in any kind of crisis is dubbed his or her "highness," and is given a crown.

If you're not sure what sort of tone you've been setting in your own workplace, just close your eyes and listen very carefully, or wander around the workplace with your eyes and ears open and your mouth shut. What do you hear? Do you hear the sounds of laughter? Are the voices of workers around you excited in a positive way? Do people look enthusiastic to be fulfilling their tasks? If you cannot see or hear a sense of joy in your workplace, you have your task cut out for you. You need to begin building a culture of fun into your department.

Don't Just Manage Change . . . Propel It!

These days, it's very popular to talk about managing change. In a lot of ways, however, this expression is an oxymoron. While change does happen, it isn't necessarily something one can manage, but something one should propel. It's up to leaders to get their teams to buy into and support the change that needs to happen. Remember, people believe in what they help create.

From the perspective of some employees, however, change can look like an undesirable challenge. It may be fear of the unknown or a preference to stay with the status quo. Obviously, some employees are more change oriented than others, but with the right leadership, most employees can come to embrace change as positive.

One way to make change more palatable is to determine employee hot buttons. You need to identify—or help them figure out——what's in it for them.

No two employees are going to respond exactly the same way when confronted with a significant change. Some people are more

Consider this hot-button activity to get employees to buy into an organizational change or initiative.

1. Describe a change or major action that you want to implement in the workplace.

2. Who do you need to influence to bring about this action?

3. Pick one of the people listed in number 2, and list three reactions that this person will most likely have to your request.

4. Write a sample scenario showing how you will state your request and how that person will answer.

naturally adaptable than others, and certain people may have to be dragged kicking and screaming in the direction of change. And without question, members of different generations may also respond differently to the prospect of change.

Not surprisingly, most Millennials tend to embrace change very enthusiastically. They're used to working quickly and under pressure, so many of them actually thrive when change is on the table. As notable multitaskers, they aren't necessarily thrown off track when a curve comes their way. As a leader, you may in fact find that dangling a change in front of your younger employees is a very effective way to motivate them. Give them a chance to implement a new procedure, develop a fresh solution, or create an original project—all of which involve bringing change to the workplace—and you should find their response enthusiastic.

Keys to Chapter 5

- No matter how cool your company may appear to Millennial job candidates, once you have them on board, it's imperative that you also provide a cool work environment. Salary, perks, and other things that may originally have drawn them to your organization aren't going to keep them loyal if they find the work to be drudgery.

- You want to make sure that promising employees get tagged as keepers—people you simply don't want to lose.

- Millennials like to feel appreciated and valued. They need to know that they are making an honest-to-goodness contribution to your organization. If they feel the work they are doing does not matter, they'll lose enthusiasm and become disengaged.

- Challenge your Millennial employees to take on more (or different) responsibilities. Toss them a challenge. Ask them to pick up the slack on an important goal or to undertake an exciting new project. The Millennial generation thrives on these types of assignments.

- Cross-train Millennial employees for other jobs throughout the organization. Some of the most innovative organizational onboarding programs place new recruits into a variety of jobs for a limited period of time before their final position in the company is determined.

- You have to have well-structured systems in place in your organization to help unproductive employees either improve their performance or to help them as they exit the company. Don't hold on to them needlessly, and don't accept marginal performance.

- There is a very critical reason your organization cannot afford to put up with mediocre employee performance: The kind of atmosphere that supports mediocrity would be a major turnoff to the keepers, your better-performing Millennials (and high performers from other generations as well).

- In an increasingly global marketplace, the awareness of different cultures is a critical component in successfully doing business. The more sensitive new employees are to these differences, the more effective they will be at recognizing and overcoming certain obstacles that diversity may cause.

- Your organization's approach to managing differences could send a powerful message to younger workers that all employees are valued for their contributions.

- To create an environment that is engaging and exciting for Millennial workers, you're going to have to determine whether your work culture truly supports fresh ideas and new thinking.

- One way to help others embrace the change you want to make is to determine your employees' hot buttons and to talk about the change in those terms. For Millennials in particular, you need to determine—or help them figure out—what's in it for them.

6

Managing Millennials

So much of what we call management consists in making it difficult for people to work.

—Peter Drucker

Contrary to some of the often-expressed frustrations of supervisors, Millennials aren't unmanageable. They certainly bring a different set of expectations with them to the workplace, and their attitudes can often seem confounding. But Millennials are superb multitaskers with plenty of energy and a propensity for teamwork. When coached properly, they make great employees and demonstrate a real potential for advancement. Managers just have to learn the most effective methods to give Millennials feedback and make corrections without demotivating them.

Corrections that Count

Unfortunately, even the best performers sometimes lose their way. To err is human. Mistakes get made. And they have to be discussed. You need to make sure that you have an effective coaching system, so you can help a good performer to get back on track. You want to make sure that your message is understood clearly, so you don't risk losing the very people you most want to keep, even when they've let you down.

The best way to have a constructive, effective coaching discussion for either positive or corrective feedback is to make sure that you follow a set of structured guidelines. These types of discussions should be precisely conducted and performed in a firm but positive tone.

Millennial employees need regular feedback on their performance. In fact, some desire continual feedback from their managers.

"We don't have the fear of being perceived as being needy," one Millennial employee shared. "We are driven and motivated, and we want to deliver what our managers want."

The idea of giving constant feedback may seem exhausting or unnecessary to the average manager, but it's exactly what Millennials say they need. Taking the time to give more feedback keeps your employees striving to do their best for your company and provides the information Millennials need for personal development.

However, the traditional prescription for delivering a corrective message may not fly with Millennials, who conversely seek large amounts of feedback but may become defensive in the face of massive amounts of negative feedback. How you frame the discussion will have a great deal to do with how well it goes over and whether you end up getting the positive changes in behavior that you are seeking.

The Model for Giving Corrective Feedback on page 105 provides a framework.

Despite the fact that the Millennial generation seeks lots of feedback, the fact also remains that Millennials prefer most of that feedback to be positive. Negative feedback is not a lot of fun for anybody, and it can be positively depressing for the younger generation. That's why it's important to make sure that you balance critical or negative feedback with positive input. If you have to tell them what they're doing wrong, also be prepared to remind them of what they are doing right. This is the best way to keep Millennial employees on track and moving in the right direction. And involve them in the solution rather than using an "I tell, you do" approach, which is a complete turn off to them.

Model for Giving Corrective Feedback

1. *The Problem*

What is usually said: "Your behavior is not acceptable. You need to quit doing _____."

*What they **want** to hear:* "You've been doing a terrific job, and I'm very happy with the results."

What you need to say: "I'm very happy with many of the things that you've been doing, such as _____. However, if you improve _____, it will be good for you and for the organization."

2. *The Consequences*

What is usually said: "You are causing problems. You have to change, or there will be consequences."

*What they **want** to hear:* "I know you had the best of intentions and that it really wasn't your fault."

What you need to say: "I understand what you intended. If you do _____, you will be more successful. Otherwise, there will be consequences, such as _____."

3. *The New Behavior(s)*

What is usually said: "Just figure it out and fix it."

*What they **want** to hear:* "I know that you know best what needs to change and that you will follow through."

What you need to say: "If you do _____, you can make a stronger impact. What are you willing to commit to?"

4. *The Follow-Up*

What is usually said: "We'll talk about this again at a later time."

*What they **want** to hear:* "I trust you to do the right thing and to make these changes as soon as you can."

What you need to say: "Let's agree to review progress on the changes that you committed to make by _____."

If You Can't Enthuse Them, Lose Them!

It's important for managers to make sure they have developed valid, reliable measures for performance and have clearly communicated those expectations to employees, so there are no surprises or misunderstandings. However, if worse comes to worse and you can't turn your employees around, you may have to face the fact you'll have no choice but to fire them. It's not a pleasant task, and few supervisors have much stomach for it. But as we previously pointed out, letting a bad apple spoil the rest of the barrel is not a great choice. Taking swift and sure action to remove the bad influence will ultimately make your job easier and will be welcomed by your other employees, who won't have to endure mediocre performance by underperforming peers any longer.

But you need to be certain that you conduct the removal of the problem employee the right way. There can be pitfalls, and you need to avoid them. When the scheduled time comes and the employee, regardless of generation, is sitting across the desk from you, be sure to adhere to the guidelines in the Dos and Don'ts box on page 107.

Once the employee is seated, take a deep breath and say what you need to say. Here is an example of the proper way to word a termination:

> As you know, John, we've met repeatedly with respect to you needing to meet your sales quota. Specifically, we've had at least seven coaching sessions previous to this. During the last coaching session, I gave you a warning that your lack of performance would lead to disciplinary actions. As such, we've had three progressive discipline meetings about your lack of performance, and during our most recent one on March 3, I gave you a written warning that unless you improved your numbers, this could end in possible termination. John, you're still not meeting your sales quota. You no longer have a job here. You are terminated immediately. I'm aware that we owe you a final paycheck and a commission check, and those will be mailed to you on the next regular payday. At this point, I need your keys to the office, company

---

Dos and Don'ts

- Do clear your desk of any distracting paperwork. You owe it to this employee to give him or her your full attention.

- Do have another person present—either someone from the human resources (HR) department or another manager—to witness the termination.

- Do remember to treat the person with dignity and respect, no matter how frustrated you are.

- Do focus on the action or lack of action on the employee's part—not what you or others did or did not do.

- Don't offer the employee coffee or water or food. You want him or her out quickly.

- Don't start the meeting with idle chitchat, such as talking about the weather, the kids, or the newest client.

- Don't chicken out. You've come this far. You just have to do it.

- Don't forget that the person has to go home and face those close to him or her.

- Don't hesitate to immediately notify the HR department or authorities if you think the employee might retaliate in some way.

---

credit card, and any other company property in your possession. Please take fifteen minutes to quietly retrieve your belongings. Bob will then escort you to your car.

Then you stop talking. Don't keep going on about why you made your decision. Don't rehash any old information you already covered during your coaching sessions or progressive-discipline sessions. Don't say another word. You have said what you had to say, and that's all you need to do.

This is what's called a "ten-minute termination." You're keeping the meeting short and to the point. Although you may experience an uncomfortable silence after the initial bad news, refrain from talking. You don't want to be there, and once the employee hears the bad news, he or she won't want to be there either, and the meeting will end quickly.

The true benefit to taking swift and sure action to remove a bad apple is that you will be left with a better organization, free of discord and substandard performance. Your remaining team members will be grateful to have a source of tension and distraction removed from their workplace (although they may not express it—loyalty dies hard).

Check Them before They Check Out

Many employers wait until an employee has turned in a resignation to ask him or her to share feelings about the organization. These exit interviews are usually gleaned for information by the human resources department to help managers understand what they need to do to keep their best employees. Talk about shutting the door after the horse has left the barn!

The time to find out how employees feel about your organization is while they are current, active, and contributing members of your team. Instead of exit interviews, your company should be conducting keeper interviews with the talented Millennials you want to retain.

Schedule regular meetings with each employee to gain an appraisal of the organization from his or her perspective. Think of it as a reverse report card: Instead of the teacher evaluating the students, the students evaluate the teacher. You might be surprised by what you could learn.

There are certain ground rules, however. You will need to make it clear that the purpose of the interview is to gather information that you need to continue to enhance your leadership and the workplace. Don't shoot the messenger!

"I was so nervous to tell my boss that I was bored on my job," one Millennial confessed. "After all, I was only on the job for three months. Once I asked for more challenges, I was given the opportunity to take on a difficult customer. I became the go-to person to solve customer issues and really felt proud about it." Your task is to listen without judgment, asking questions only for clarification. Try not to get drawn into a debate, but don't be afraid to explain something that the employee may be unclear on, such as promotion policies or company programs. Again, the goal is to gather information, not to engage in debate.

A list of sample keeper-interview questions follows.

Sample Keeper-Interview Questions

- What's working well for you?
- Where are your current challenges?
- Of what recent accomplishment are you most proud?
- What would you like to learn or do next?
- How can I best support you?

Give 'Em a High Five—Often!

Some organizations dole out praise so sparingly, one would think it was rarer than uranium! But if you want to create a dynamic workplace, you're going to have to learn to be liberal with acknowledgments. For Millennials, in particular, the frequency of positive feedback is important to them.

It doesn't cost a lot of money and it doesn't take a lot of time to let your employees know when they've done something right. The closer your feedback is to the point at which the employee made the accomplishment, the stronger the positive reinforcement, even though time and distance sometimes make it difficult to give an on-the-spot compliment.

As we've noted before, the Millennials are accustomed to receiving lots of praise and plenty of pats on the back. They were raised by parents who believed in the value of positive feedback and who went out of their way to make sure their children developed a strong sense of self-esteem. The Millennials' teachers were also taught to provide lots of reinforcement as a more effective means of instruction.

All this adds up to a generation that is more powered by a pat on the back than a kick in the butt! Most employees can easily conjure up memories of corrective feedback discussions, especially since many of them are highly structured, focused, and intense. Although the pats on the back may in fact be given more frequently, they are often quick and sporadic, without the lasting memory of a job well done.

The fact remains that if you want to see positive behaviors being repeated on the job, you have to use positive reinforcement with your employees. And just as with corrective discussions, the more structured you make the feedback, the more effective it is in producing the repeated behaviors that you find desirable.

One of the great things about watching team sports— soccer, rugby, football, and others—is seeing the effectiveness of positive reinforcement when it is delivered on the spot after a significant accomplishment. Team members celebrate each other's accomplishments. They applaud, cheer, and high-five their teammates when something victorious occurs. It's one of the reasons why we love sports, and it should be one of the reasons why we love successful employees!

When you are prepared to give your Millennial employees positive feedback (and be prepared to do that often with younger workers), there are certain rules to follow that will help make the feedback all that more effective. See Guidelines for Positive Feedback box on page 111.

Hire "Can" and "Will" Employees

Obviously, not all of your Millennial employees will be alike. No matter how well educated they are, or even how experienced, some incoming recruits are going to have a difficult time becoming

Guidelines for Positive Feedback

- *Be as specific as possible.*

Generic feedback isn't worth the paper it's printed on! Telling an employee to keep up the good work is just not specific enough. However, telling an employee what he or she did well and specifically why it was effective is the ideal way to reinforce behavior you wish to see repeated.

- *Discuss the ramifications.*

Don't count on employees to understand the big picture. Just because you compliment their efforts doesn't mean they understand how that contributes to the bottom line. Take the time to educate them on how their behavior has a payoff for the organization.

- *Ask for feedback.*

This isn't a one-way conversation if you're smart. Give your employee a chance to discuss how he or she accomplished the success. It's a great way of reinforcing his or her efforts and building confidence.

- *Tell them thanks.*

Most of the time, the two words that employees seldom hear—which can have a profound effect—are "thank you." Try them. These two words can work wonders!

productive employees. Your job as a manager in recruiting Millennial candidates is to make sure that you make job offers to those who *can* and *will* be able to learn the job.

Look for people who have the natural gifts and proper training necessary to become competent in the position. These are "cans," as opposed to "can'ts," who lack the talents and skills to achieve competency. "Wills" are those people who are positive and optimistic, bringing a natural enthusiasm to new experiences. "Won'ts" are those who are inflexible and tend to resist new experiences.

This is where it's important to "go slow to go fast" to make sure you are hiring candidates with the right fit. Better to take your time in selecting the right candidate than to hurry through the process and take back steps to re-recruit and rehire.

No manager likes to bring employees into the organization that lack the fundamentals to do the job, but you don't always have a choice in the skill levels of the people you interview. Some talent pools are deeper than others, after all. In most cases, you are much better off to hire a less-skilled person who is willing to learn, as opposed to hiring someone with what appears to be a negative attitude or resistance to change.

As one Millennial said:

> I remember being interviewed by a department head. The first thing he said to me was, "I have been working at this company longer than you have been alive," and my thought bubble was, "So what?" I was so intimidated by this man, yet I worked hard in the interview to make sure he knew how willing I was to learn whatever I needed to be excellent in the job. He hired me. Over time, I earned his respect, and he rewarded me with bigger projects and more responsibilities.

Millennials were reared on a "you can do anything" attitude. It is imperative that leaders hire those Millennials who can speak to both their "can" and "will" capabilities—including any evidence of where and when they have called upon these behaviors in former school and work situations. It's important for leaders to model a positive attitude and enthusiasm for learning.

Demonstrate the behavior and hold others accountable to the following:

- Be receptive to learning something new.

- Appreciate what you have and where you are.
- Have a vision of how you want to succeed.
- Set goals to accomplish your vision.
- See value in new experiences—even difficult ones.
- Imagine a positive outcome.
- Use doubt as a strategy for gathering information (ask questions).
- Try to look at existing circumstances in a new way, through a different frame.
- Take responsibility for outcomes.
- Get as much information as possible.
- Keep physically and mentally fit.
- Utilize inner resources, such as creativity, focus, courage, discipline, humor, and perspective.

These behaviors serve leaders well when they coach and manage Millennials on a regular basis.

Remember to Celebrate Wins

One of the most important roles of leaders is to make sure that their teams recognize success. This might seem an obvious expectation, but you would be surprised by how many leaders almost forget to focus on accomplishments. So, in addition to putting goals in writing—using specific terms and concrete measures—it's important for leaders to confirm their accomplishments by celebrating employee successes.

These may be individual successes or team successes. Not only do these celebrations serve as a necessary pat on the back, but they also tend to reinforce the organization's mission. In a lot of organizations, of course, the process of celebrating victories is very formal. In other organizations, success celebrations might be as simple as an employee-of-the-month award program. In still others, they could take the form of nothing more than informal congratulations or personal notes from managers.

A recognition activity that you can use with your team follows.

You're a Star!

Objective: To recognize team member strengths and contributions.

Audience: Any size.

Time: 10 minutes.

Process:

1. Ask each person to print his or her name in large letters on a piece of 8.5" × 11" cardstock and hang the card in the room.

2. Give each person a stack of five to ten star-shaped Post-it notes.

3. Ask participants to look around the room and identify something they want to acknowledge about a team member's talents, achievements, or measures of support. Participants write what they appreciate about five to ten team members, listing one talent, achievement, or measure of support on each of the Post-it notes.

4. Ask participants to then distribute their Post-it notes to each recipient and orally tell the recipient what they appreciate about him or her.

5. Have recipients place their Post-it notes on their displayed piece of cardstock.

6. Individuals can walk around the room to view each other's Post-it notes.

But however you choose to celebrate successes, you have to find some way to "ring a bell" when an employee does something right. The concept here is that success breeds success. Recognition leads to renewed efforts. If you allow employees' successes to go unrecognized or to be taken for granted, you risk discouraging your team and seeing successes begin to dwindle. And remember, Millennials' parents celebrated everything: graduation from kindergarten, entrance to middle school, participating in (and not even necessarily winning) a spelling bee, and every other achievement, no matter how small. They are used to accolades and acknowledgments for both efforts and results.

Another benefit of being the type of leader who frequently celebrates successes is that you become known as a players' manager—the type of leader who tends to put employees first. That's a good reputation to have! This is one way to attract the best and the brightest to your department or division.

And let's face it: Even the most successful teams can falter every now and then. Loudly and publicly celebrating the team's success can be a very effective way to get it back on track. It's a great motivating tool. One client company developed tool kits for managers and loaded them with items to be used for recognition and celebration, which included things such as Post-it notes, thank-you cards, gift cards, stamps, stars, tiaras, and crowns.

Finally, successful leaders need to think of themselves in multidimensional ways. Sometimes, it's your job to be the coach. At other times, your job may be to do nothing more than referee. And even perhaps more frequently, you need to see your job as being a cheerleader for your employees. If you become their biggest fan, they will soon become your biggest supporters.

Elevate Communication to an Art Form

Over the course of 30 years in the practice of consulting, we've worked with hundreds of organizations. Perhaps not surprisingly, the biggest problem afflicting the majority of those organizations was poor communication. Sometimes, the problem was from the top down. Other times, it was from the bottom up. And from time to time, it was across departmental lines. But no matter what the source of poor communication is, it's a factor that affects everything that an organization does.

Even worse, sometimes when an organization suffers from communication problems, the precise cause of the difficulty isn't always apparent. We have worked with many organizations that took great pains to put out lots of information. They conducted meetings and produced newsletters, e-mails, brochures, manuals, web sites, and numerous other forms of communication, yet still failed to connect with employees.

It sometimes can be mystifying when trying to figure out why employees just don't get it! Typically, however, the problem is that management just doesn't get it. The leadership team that doesn't listen to its employees—that isn't in touch with what employees think or how they feel—isn't going to be able to maintain effective communication.

One of the biggest areas of concern revolves around the organization's vision. Most of the CEOs that we've worked with have been frustrated because the front line seemed so disconnected from the vision of the organization. Who's responsible? Clearly, it's a leadership problem.

The Mature generation, and to a lesser extent, the Baby Boomer generation, were both more accustomed to following marching orders. As the old saying goes among soldiers (courtesy of *The Charge of the Light Brigade*), "Ours is not to reason why, ours is but to do or die." But, even members of the older generations have a natural curiosity about where the organization is going and what their role within it will be.

When it comes to the Millennial generation, however, communication is hypercritical. Younger workers may well be unable to function if they can't see the bigger picture. How can they

Describing the Big Picture

- Describe the major initiatives that are most important within your business group.

- Explain how business group initiatives support the overall organizational vision.

- Describe the advantages and challenges that you and your team will face while working toward those initiatives (strengths, weaknesses, opportunities, and threats).

- Indicate why you feel these initiatives are important.

- Identify the key elements of each person's position responsibilities that support the accomplishment of the business group's initiatives.

- Discuss the behaviors that are critical for the accomplishment of the business group initiatives.

- Ask employees to think about ways to hold each other accountable for accomplishing the group's initiatives.

contribute if they don't understand the ultimate direction? The tool in the box above, Describing the Big Picture, will help provide this.

New recruits from among the Millennials will make it very clear from the beginning that they expect frequent communications from their managers. They're used to being communicated with in detail by both parents and teachers, so they won't take kindly to the feeling of being kept in the dark.

It's not uncommon for employers that have active exit-interview programs to discover that many departing employees simply didn't grasp how their job contributed to the organization's success. Combine that with lack of direct feedback on performance, and you have a recipe for high turnover.

"The biggest complaint I get from Millennial employees in their exit interviews is that nobody told them how they were doing," shared one HR professional. "Millennial employees need a lot of feedback. They want to know how they are doing now, then again in two days, and then again at the end of the week."

Be mindful that the failure to communicate costs the corporation money. How much revenue is lost by corporations each year due to a lack of clarity in communications? It's hard to measure, for sure, but mistakes, reworking, and time lost due to poor communication all lead to dollars lost.

Definitely Switch It Up

Since the Millennial generation prefers a mix of work tasks and a variety of responsibilities, you have to be wary of placing them into a routine job. The prospect of routine work is drudgery to most Millennials. It won't take long to lose their interest and enthusiasm if the work seems boring and mundane.

One manager shared:

> The Millennials I work with, whether they are college graduates or not, share one thing in common: They are extremely impatient. They believe they should get what they want and on their timeline. For example, I have been working closely with a clerical employee to help establish a realistic timeline for her to learn her job and then eventually be promoted and transferred to another department. Just today, she marched into my office and said that she wants to be transferred *now*, instead of following the timeline we agreed upon. As a result, I have been called into a last-minute meeting to discuss her desire to be transferred. If she is, I will also need to find and train a new employee to replace her.

And as one Millennial stated:

> The reason I left my previous employer is because I was not moving up fast enough. The company had identified me as a future leader and spent money to send me to leadership development training. My managers and I had a lot of conversations about my desire for a leadership role,

yet they chose not to act. I waited two years for a promotion. I was very vocal that I wanted a change. My managers were not surprised when I left the company.

One way around this dilemma is to make sure that you switch things up for younger workers. Try to vary their job responsibilities, especially as a way of responding to current business conditions or to new demands of the marketplace.

One Millennial, who works as a marketing manager in a small start-up company, states:

> I love my job. My boss gives me all kinds of opportunities I wouldn't have in a very large corporation. I've volunteered to learn desktop publishing to develop our marketing brochures. I've traveled to Iowa to review our packaging and to select the most attractive display. I was part of a very successful product launch to secure a new market segment that has brought in a quarter of our revenues. Even though some of my friends make more money, they are all envious of the experiences I've been given. My job rocks!

Job sharing—two people sharing the same position—may also be an effective strategy. Another technique is to put Millennials into special, temporary project teams, each working part of the week. But either way you do it, you're going to need to make sure your Millennial employees are fully challenged and not falling into the pit of minutia.

Leaders aren't always aware when their employees have reached a threshold of boredom. However, you can always count on the Millennials to come to you and ask for some form of job enrichment. Your best bet is to survey them to find out what turns them on when it comes to work and what bores them to tears. Use the Talent Survey tool on page 120 to assess your current team member.

The results of the survey should help open your eyes to which parts of the job employees find challenging and which parts they find stultifying. Armed with this information, you may be able to reassign job responsibilities or to work on revamping procedures.

Talent Survey

1. Currently, I am most interested in the opportunity to: _____

2. I get the most satisfaction from: _____

3. I am a quick study when it comes to: _____

4. I have been most successful when I: _____

5. I sometimes struggle with: _____

6. I usually avoid doing: _____

Take a fresh look at work rules and job procedures with your Millennials. There's always more than one way to do things, and there's certainly more than one way for any employee to get the job done. Remain open-minded and allow your employees to tell you where they see the opportunities for improvement and streamlining.

Finally, as a leader, you're going to find that the influx of Millennial employees into your department or division over the next few years may well open your eyes. Even though good management practices are timeless and not generationally dependent, your younger workers are likely to be more demanding and will bring higher expectations to the workplace.

Despite some of the inevitable conflicts that could arise, look at Millennials as a challenge to your management skills and as an opportunity to become a better leader. They will test you, without question, and they may doubt you. You may even doubt yourself at times. But if you take a constructive approach and make a concerted effort to fully engage them, the overall impact on your entire organization could be extremely positive and motivating.

Keys to Chapter 6

- The traditional prescription for delivering a corrective message may not fly with Millennials, who conversely seek large amounts of feedback but may become defensive in the face of massive amounts of negative feedback.

- Managers need to carefully give Millennials feedback regarding corrections they need to make without demotivating them.

- It's important for managers to make sure they have developed valid, reliable measures for performance and have clearly communicated those expectations to employees, so there are no surprises or misunderstandings.

- Taking swift and sure action to remove underperforming employees will ultimately make your job easier and will be welcomed by your other employees, who won't have to endure another's mediocre performance.

- The time to find out how employees feel about your organization is while they are current, active, contributing members of your team. Instead of exit interviews, your company should be conducting keeper interviews with those talented Millennials you want to stay.

- If you want to see positive behaviors being repeated on the job, you have to use positive reinforcement with your employees. And just as with corrective discussions, the more structured you make the feedback, the more effective it is in producing the repeated behaviors that you find desirable.

- Your job as a manager in recruiting Millennial candidates is to make sure that you make job offers to those who *can* and *will* be able to learn the job. This is where it's important to "go slow to go fast" to make sure you are hiring candidates with the right fit.

- The "cans" and "wills" are those who have a positive attitude, enthusiasm, skills (or know how to obtain them), and abilities.

"Cans" and "wills" are people who rate highly in both capability and willingness to take on a task.

- One of the most important roles of leaders is to make sure that their followers recognize success. So, in addition to putting goals in writing—using specific terms and concrete measures—it's important for leaders to confirm employees' accomplishments by celebrating their successes.

- When it comes to the Millennial generation, communication is hypercritical. Younger workers may well be unable to function if their leaders don't communicate the bigger picture.

- Be mindful that the failure to communicate costs the corporation money. Mistakes, reworking, and time lost caused by miscommunication all lead to dollars lost.

- Take a fresh look at work rules and job procedures with your Millennials. There's always more than one way to do things, and there's certainly more than one way for any employee to get the job done.

7

Millennial or Boomer?

> We turn not older with years, but newer every day.
>
> —Emily Dickinson

Similarities that Bridge the Generations

We have written much about the differences between Millennials and other generations, but let's not forget about the similarities. Think of it this way: In addition to calling them "Millennials" and "Generation Y," these young people are also sometimes called "Echo Boomers." While the term originally was meant to refer to the size of their generation (which is larger than the Baby Boomer generation before them), it may also imply something more. Millennials may actually be thought of as "Echo Boomers" because they are remarkably similar to their parents in many ways.

We can see similarities between Millennials and Boomers in their relationships with technology, their passion for music, and their shared values related to success, hard work, diversity, and freedom, among others.

The Age of Technology

Another term sometimes applied to the Millennial generation is "Cyber Kids." This is fitting, since no generation in history has been as pervasively and intensely exposed to new technology than they have been. In contrast, Boomers are often thought of as being somewhat technically challenged. Without doubt, the *Computers for Dummies* and *Computers for Complete Idiots* books were primarily geared to the post–World War II generation. But it would be misleading to think that technology didn't also define the upbringing of the Boomer generation.

For example, while Millennials came of age during what can only be called a true technological explosion, it was the Boomers who were raised at the leading edge of a significant boom in post–World War II technology.

And speaking as two members of the Baby Boomer generation, let us not forget that the computer technology that has so revolutionized the world of the twenty-first century was developed by twentieth-century Boomer entrepreneurs such as Steve Jobs, Steve Wozniak, Bill Gates, Paul Allen, and many others. It would be truly misleading to think that the post–World War II generation was in some way antitechnology or technology adverse.

Take television, for instance. The expansion of television primarily occurred following World War II, during the childhood period of Boomers. Around the world, Boomers grew up with shows like *Howdy Doody, Monty Python's Flying Circus, Danger Man,* and *Tinderbox.* Television in its infancy period was raw and somewhat unsophisticated, but it was captivating, informing, and motivating. Some parents of the Boomers thought it was the best babysitter that money could buy!

Television for the Millennials, of course, was a richer experience with infinitely more choices. They grew up with *Sesame Street, Teletubbies, Mister Rogers' Neighborhood, Babar,* and *Paddington Bear,* as well as MTV, BBC, CNN, and choices galore. But for both generations, TV was no less captivating, entertaining, or motivating.

Millennials and Boomers also share a fondness for instant images. Today, cameras can be found in everything from computers to cell phones, and digital cameras are all the rage, which has led to a profusion of web sites for the uploading and sharing of digital images. Photo prints are now routinely made from digital sources rather than film negatives.

While Boomers enjoyed nothing like the extensive access to photographs and videos that Millennials enjoy, it could be argued that the roots of a widespread interest in instant photo imagery can be traced to the childhood years of the Baby Boomers.

The Polaroid camera, in its own time, was just as revolutionary as today's digital photography. It freed picture takers from the time constraints of having film developed and printed, thus leading to an explosion of interest in quick and candid film photography that lasted up until the advent of digital photography. And let's not forget that it was Boomer parents—anxious to capture every step, smile, and hiccup of their offspring for posterity—that drove the camera market. Clearly, video cameras and digital photography were a boon to the enthusiasm of Boomer parents.

The Medium Is the Message

And speaking of digital images, Boomers and Millennials also share a common orientation to document management and image manipulation.

By the time Boomers first began entering the workplace, electric typewriters and office copiers had become commonplace. Most Baby Boomers are old enough to remember a time when producing copies of a typed document required layers of messy carbon paper. It limited the types of copies that could be made and distributed (although it might have resulted in several million *fewer* memos being distributed throughout businesses everywhere). Then, along came IBM Selectric typewriters and Xerox machines!

Boomers took to this new technology willingly, and quickly learned how to copy, scale, duplex, and collate elaborate business and academic documents. These tools—the copier and the electric type-writer—actually proved to be creative resources that gave their users greater control over printed communications (even if the paper blob infested most offices and overflowed most file cabinets).

For Millennials, the equivalent communication technology has been the personal computer, scanner, and printer. Armed with these tools, Millennials eagerly produce colorful, high-quality term papers, reports, and presentations. Even if the Millennials have an edge in technology having grown up with it, and even if many Boomers continue to struggle keeping up with evolving technology, both Boomers and Millennials appreciate the value of these electronic tools to communicate complex information.

While the specific technologies that are most familiar to each generation may *seem* to have different roots, both Boomers and Millennials came of age during technological revolutions that seemed to define their generations. Even if the technologies are different, that affinity for putting technology to practical use is a common thread between the generations.

Words and Music

In addition to television, the 1960s and 1970s also presented Baby Boomers with music technology that proved to be a game changer for the music industry. The mid-1960s saw the introduction of eight-track tapes, which were a convenient and secure way to listen to purchased music (from the recording industry's standpoint).

The advent of small cassette tape recorders, on the other hand, placed the control of music *directly* into the hands of the end user for the first time in a widespread way. The user could make and share copies or record off the radio, all without paying for the music. The music industry was so alarmed at the potential for tape recorders to cut into the sales of records, they took legal steps and had the law changed to prohibit tape-recording published music.

Similarly, the online music-sharing site Napster made it possible for Millennials to digitally record and share their music collections online without paying royalties to the artists or record companies. The Recording Industry Association of America went after Napster with a barrage of lawsuits, eventually putting the college-student-created web site out of business. Napster eventually returned under a paid-royalty arrangement, but by then, the genie was out of the bottle. Today, Millennials share their music digitally as freely as their parents did using cassette tapes.

The Music Goes Round and Round!

Nothing seemed to separate the Boomer generation from their WWII-era parents more sharply than rock 'n' roll music. Even while both generations were viewing Elvis's shocking performance on *The Ed Sullivan Show*, with studio cameras focused firmly above the King's hips, Boomers were beginning to swing to a beat that the world had never seen. It was truly revolutionary and forever defined a new era in history.

As one friend of ours explained to his teenage daughter a few years ago, "You don't seem to understand something. We Baby Boomers are the coolest parents in the history of parents. We invented rock 'n' roll!"

Yet, in many ways, the generational music gap still exists. Boomer parents don't always understand the music their Millennial offspring download. But the music of today defines the Millennial generation to a certain extent, just as the music of their generation defined Baby Boomers.

In the 1960s and early 1970s, the sounds of several different genres blared from transistor radios and tape decks, including pop music, folk music, rock, rhythm and blues, Motown, jazz, country, and gospel. Vinyl records were the medium of choice until cassette tapes began to predominate in the late 1960s. By the early 1980s, digital recording began to surface in the form of compact discs.

Unfortunately, that meant many Boomers had to buy a copy of the Beatles' "White album" for the third time!

But as the Boomer generation began to marry and start families, styles and tastes of music began to evolve further. The late 1970s and early 1980s gave rise to the disco sound, punk music, rap, glam rock, heavy metal, reggae, and alternative country. And it was just at the end of this era that the very youngest of the Millennial generation began to take an interest in pop music. For many, that meant that the New Kids on the Block began to replace *Sesame Street*'s Elmo!

But the 1990s also began to see the emergence of forms of music that were truly new: techno, house, ska, emo, screamo, metalcore, grunge, and the improbable return of bubblegum pop in the form of Britney Spears and Christina Aguilera.

The Tunes They Are a Changin'

While the music genres may have been different, Millennials, like their parents before them, used music to bond socially, express complex emotions, and define the world around them.

A Baby Boomer friend of ours was driving his daughter to a soccer match one day many years ago when a song came on the radio with the lyrics from "Iris" by the Goo Goo Dolls: "And I don't want the world to see me, 'cause I don't think that they'd understand. When everything's made to be broken, I just want you to know who I am." Hearing the lyric, his daughter said, "Daddy, that's exactly how I feel sometimes." She was seven years old at the time!

For Boomers, though, song lyrics also carried a great deal of meaning. During their youth, a cavalcade of talented artists gave voice to their deepest feelings: Elvis Presley, the Beatles, Diana Ross and the Supremes, the Who, the Beach Boys, the Temptations, Michael Jackson, the Rolling Stones, Elton John, Bruce Springsteen, the Tielman Brothers, Aretha Franklin, and many, many others. For Millennials, a new breed of artists also spoke to their hearts, such as

Nirvana, Eminem, Pearl Jam, Puff Daddy, Mariah Carey, the Spice Girls, and the Backstreet Boys.

Despite differences in the number and type of genres, and despite obvious differences in their favorite artists, the feelings quite often expressed in music are similar. Just compare Nirvana's song "Smells Like Teen Spirit" with the Rolling Stones classic "I Can't Get No Satisfaction," and you'll hear the echo of very similar fears and frustrations.

To be sure, the methods of music delivery are also much different now than they were 40 years ago, and the number of genres Millennials listen to can be bewildering. But the love of music for both generations is a common thread that binds them together more often than you might think.

For example, it has been noted that the Millennials may be the first generation in history that truly likes and admires much of their parent's music. Seminal rock musicians such as the Beatles, the Rolling Stones, Jim Morrison, Eric Clapton, and many others are just as popular among Millennials today as they have been among their parents. By the same token, it isn't unusual for Baby Boomer parents to accompany their children to concerts by younger artists, such as Miley Cyrus, or for Millennials to accompany their parents to a Stones concert. Just try to imagine Baby Boomers attending a Lawrence Welk concert with their folks or dragging their parents to a Led Zepplin bash!

In another respect, both generations have defined their era with particular songs by popular artists. Even though the majority of Baby Boomers were not hippies or counterculture warriors, songs such as "Blowing in the Wind," "I Can't Get No Satisfaction," "The Times They Are a Changing," "Revolution," "The Eve of Destruction," and "Don't Let Me Be Misunderstood" clearly spoke to the conscience of that generation.

Many Millennials also see the lyrics of thought-provoking music as defining their generation. Recent examples include "Runaway

Love" by Ludacris (featuring Mary J. Blige), which tells the stories of three young girls fleeing abusive situations. Another song, "If Everyone Cared" by Nickelback, is a lively rock song that calls for civic engagement. And "Let Love In" by the Goo Goo Dolls is featured in a pop-rock video that touches on genocide, poverty, and global warming.

It's probably no more common for Boomers and Millennials to compare music lyrics today than it was for Boomers and their Big Band–listening parents to compare notes 40 years ago. But Boomers and Millennials should be better able to bridge any music gap that exists just by keeping an open mind.

What You Are Is *Still* What You Were

One of the most frequent complaints that seems to be leveled at Millennial employees concerns their supposed lack of a work ethic. Usually, when an older worker confronts a newer, younger worker in a new setting—such as an office or factory floor—differences in values become the first and most apparent conflict that arises. It's only natural that different generations reflect different sets of values, considering that they grew up in different eras under a different set of circumstances.

Those differences and how they came to be have long been recognized by Dr. Morris Massey, a business and marketing professor who wrote the seminal work on this subject. Massey proposed that all human beings go through a similar set of phases in which their values are formed, based on the events and experiences that surround them. Further, Massey suggested that if we want to understand the differences between generations, we only have to look at the differences in those events that most impacted them as they were growing up. These may be great events that affect millions, or they may be individual experiences, such as the death of a parent, a new love, or an unexpected relocation of the family.[1]

For Boomers, the background history of their lives is rich, with a great many major milestones, including:

- Sputnik
- The Vietnam War
- The building of the Berlin Wall
- The Cuban Missile Crisis
- The assassination of John F. Kennedy
- The assassination of Dr. Martin Luther King Jr.
- The Apollo 11 moon landing
- Watergate

For Millennials, even their shorter span of time is filled with significant historical events, including:

- The space shuttle Challenger explosion
- The collapse of communism
- The fall of the Berlin Wall
- The first Gulf War
- The death of Princess Diana
- The Columbine school shooting
- The 9/11 terrorist attacks
- The Iraq War

When comparing Boomers and Millennials, it is safe to say that, on the one hand, the two generations have experienced *different* significant events, both personally as well as generally. However, because the Boomer and Millennial generations overlap, there may also be certain significant societal events that both generations share as emotional touch points. The 9/11 terrorist attacks would be a classic example of this.

Members of every generation can point to major events that have become common touch points in shared memory. Sometimes, those events are unique to a given generation, but there are also many shared moments in history that bridge two generations. Our ability to share a moment in time binds us together and reinforces common values that we all share, despite the generational gulf that may sometimes seem to divide us.

Caution . . . Your Values Are Showing

In previous chapters, we discussed how Millennial employees may often bring a different set of values to the work environment that could make it difficult to both understand and manage them effectively. We have tried to explain how many of the influences on the generation have led to different mindsets when compared with their veteran Baby Boomer coworkers.

At first glance, the differences may seem more obvious, especially when conflicts arise. But we must remember that Millennials were raised by Baby Boomers, too. Thus, this particular team of parents and children may enjoy a level of closeness and comfort rarely enjoyed by previous sets of generations. When you take a closer look at Millennials in the workplace, you realize that when it comes to values, Millennials are more like Boomers than you may think. Consider their shared values in these six areas:

- **Success**—Boomers were committed to climbing the ladder of success from the first day they set foot in their new jobs. For that ambition, there are obvious rewards, including status, money, and independence. Millennials grew up receiving heaps of positive reinforcement and being intensely groomed by their success-oriented parents for bigger and better things. Boomers desired success. Millennials expect it. And both value it.
- **Hard work**—It's often been said that Baby Boomers are notorious workaholics. They view the hard work as necessary to move up to the next level of success. But the Millennials, despite their reputation, also work hard when they are focused

and motivated. They may prefer to work on their time and in their comfort zone, but they do what it takes to get the job done. They've been doing that since facing stacks of homework in school. However, their goal to work hard may be less about moving up the ladder and more about simply finding quicker ways to get work done so they can do other things.

- **Diversity**—The Baby Boomer generation, which lived through the civil rights era, supports the concept of inclusion. Millennials, on the other hand, grew up during a period when diversity was heavily emphasized and deeply valued. They were taught about diverse people and different cultures through their education and through the media, so they have come to expect differences as part of the natural order.

- **Teamwork**—Baby Boomers entered the workforce under the supervision of the Mature generation, which preferred a top-down hierarchical style of managing. In reaction to this rigid style, the Baby Boomers actively supported teamwork as the best way to get things done without resorting to autocratic management. The Millennials are used to doing things in groups, from school to sports to dating, and as a group, they truly value collaboration.

- **Freedom**—Many members of the Boomer generation resisted "the establishment" and "the system," so they've developed a somewhat low tolerance for arbitrary rules and regulations. The Millennial generation is also skeptical of arbitrary rules and regulations, but only because they have constantly been challenged to think for themselves, and they simply don't appreciate rules just for the sake of having them.

- **Money**—The Boomer generation pioneered the two-income family, which enabled most of them to enjoy a higher standard of living than their parents could ever have dreamed of. Clearly, money is important to Baby Boomers. Since most of the children of the Baby Boomer generation grew up in this atmosphere of affluence, they tend to place high value on their earning power.

We Can Change the World

The values just described revolve around an individual's personal efforts and accomplishments. However, many of the values that Millennials and Boomers share also pertain to the individual's role in society, along with basic beliefs about what is right and wrong and how one can give back to society.

Many experts have said there's a very strong streak of idealism in the Millennial generation. Logically, many people seem to think that they picked up this trait from their Boomer parents.

There is little doubt that Millennials have been exposed to idealistic beliefs, such as community service and diversity. But their brand of idealism may not be identical to the passions that drove so many Boomers. And while there may be a fair degree of similarity in how Boomers and Millennials tend to view their social and civic obligations, it has recently been suggested that any similarities or differences in idealism between the generations is actually part of a larger cycle that reaches back nearly 200 years.

Writing in the *Washington Post,* authors Eric Greenberg and Karl Weber say that the Millennial generation is actually more "post-idealistic" and may prove to be more civic-minded in their idealism.

As they explain:

American history suggests that about every 80 years, a civic (or Joshua) generation emerges to make over the country after a period of upheaval caused by the fervor of an idealist (or Moses) generation. In 1828, 1860, 1896, 1932, and 1968, as members of new generations—alternately idealist and civic—began to vote in large numbers, the United States experienced major political shifts. This year, the civic-minded Millennials, born between 1982 and 2003, are coming of age and promising to turn the political landscape, currently defined by idealist Baby Boomers such as Clinton and George W. Bush, upside down.[2]

Although Greenberg and Weber cite American events, similar trends can be seen in world history. Examples include the European revolutions of 1848, the rise of labor unions in the late nineteenth century, the rise of socialism in Russia in 1920, the rise of fascism in Europe in the 1920s and 1930s, and the 1968 barricades throughout France and Europe. Also to the list of idealist Baby Boomers, we might add Britain's Tony Blair, France's Nicolas Sarkozy, and Germany's Angela Merkel.

During the late 1960s and early 1970s, the issues that seemed to ignite the idealism of significant numbers of Boomers were sharply defined: war, civil rights, social justice, and equality. The causes of the early twenty-first century aren't nearly as clear-cut to the Millennial generation, despite the incidence of wars, terrorism, and economic volatility.

A recent report called "Millennials Talk Politics: A Study of College Student Political Engagement" found that the younger generation struggles to identify with a particular political party or movement, let alone a particular presidential candidate. The study went on to say, "They do have goals and want to improve the world. The problem is that they're not sure whether the current political environment makes any of that possible."[3]

Greenberg and Weber agreed, adding that the Millennial generation is pragmatic in their idealism:

> Determined to find their own solutions to the major problems we face, and convinced that their unprecedented levels of education and technological know-how will enable them to do so, [the Millennial generation] shares a social orientation that might best be described in terms of what they have left behind. Speaking broadly, [they are] post-ideological, post-partisan, and post-political. They're post-ideological because they're uninterested in defending specifically "conservative" or "liberal" approaches to national problems. Instead, they're pragmatic, open-minded, and innovation-oriented, eager to experiment with new solutions no matter where they may come from.[4]

So, Millennials and Boomers both tend to be idealistic and civic-minded by nature, even though they may differ in how those characteristics are put into practice in the real world. Let's look at how those idealistic impulses play out in terms of community service, political activism, and social responsibility.

Reach Out and Touch

When President John F. Kennedy challenged the nation in 1960 to "ask not what your country can do for you, ask what you can do for your country," that call was enthusiastically answered by the first wave of Baby Boomers. The Peace Corps, founded in 1961, sent more than 14,500 volunteers to more than 50 countries around the globe. Similarly, when Volunteers in Service to America (VISTA) was created in 1964, thousands of young people spread out across America to help impoverished neighborhoods. These programs and others like them illustrate the type of hands-on idealism that drove many members of the Boomer generation.

The same sense of community spirit also moves the Millennial generation, although the forms are somewhat different. Certainly, the VISTA program (now called AmeriCorps) and the Peace Corps still exist, and they still draw young people into volunteer service. But unlike their Boomer predecessors, the vast majority of Millennials were expected to volunteer a certain number of hours of community service. Whether willingly, this younger generation looked for ways to make the world—at least their local neighborhood—a better place in which to live. And many of these students continue to provide community service, even after the required hours have been met.

So, the spirit of volunteerism and community service are values shared by members of both generations.

The concept of corporate social responsibility became a very hot topic in the 1960s, as public and elected officials began to hold large corporations accountable for actions that were perceived as harmful to the general populace. Employment policies, on-the-job safety, environmental damage, and community investment were all fair game for protests and legal action. Litigation revealed unsafe practices in everything from food dye to cigarettes to toxic waste disposal. As a result, consumer advocacy became commonplace in the 1970s and 1980s.

Millennials have grown up in an era in which the majority of organizations are expected to embrace their role in society as good citizens. Having been taught to value community service, this young generation has a preconceived sense of the type of social conscience they expect from any company they choose to work for. Wherever possible, they show a preference for employment with an organization that also engages in community service, creates good products or offers quality services, engages in green practices, and permits employees an opportunity to volunteer time or services.

For both generations, it seems as if they view employment as something more than simply drawing a paycheck. And both Boomers and Millennials expect work to be fulfilling on many levels—not just financial—and that includes having a sense of pride about the type of company they work for. Corporate social responsibility gathered steam during the 1960s and 1970s and continues to be a factor in making any organization attractive to both Boomers and Millennials.

When we talk about Millennials and Boomers, we have to face the fact that we are necessarily dealing with generalities. There's nothing wrong with that, so long as our purpose is to try to develop a broad understanding of the differences that can exist between two generations. Making assumptions such as these can be a useful way to understand and resolve conflict.

But we must be careful not to let broad assumptions mask the many similarities that exist between Millennials and their Boomer predecessors. Differences in style can usually be worked out, if not actually dismissed. Differences in substance can be worked out through listening and reasoned discussion. But our similarities must be recognized and celebrated wherever possible. They can be a source of sharing and binding that helps members of each generation bring out the best in each other.

Keys to Chapter 7

- We can see similarities between Millennials and Boomers in their relationships with technology, their passion for music, and their shared values related to success, hard work, diversity, and freedom, among others.
- While the specific technologies that are most familiar to each generation may *seem* to have different roots, both Boomers and Millennials came of age during technological revolutions that seemed to define their generations. Even if the technologies are different, that affinity for putting technology to practical use is a common thread between the generations.
- The online music-sharing site Napster made it possible for Millennials to digitally record and share their music collections online without paying royalties to the artists or record companies. Today, Millennials share their music digitally as freely as their parents did using cassette tapes.
- In the 1960s and early 1970s, the sounds of several different genres blared from transistor radios and tape decks, including pop music, folk music, rock, rhythm and blues, Motown, jazz, country, and gospel. Vinyl records were the medium of choice until cassette tapes began to predominate in the late 1960s. By the early 1980s, digital recording began to surface in the form of compact discs.
- The feelings quite often expressed in Boomer music and Millennial music are similar. Just compare Nirvana's song "Smells Like Teen Spirit" with the Rolling Stones classic "I Can't Get No Satisfaction," and you'll hear the echo of very similar fears and frustrations.
- If we want to understand the differences between generations, we only have to look at the differences in those events that most impacted them as they were growing up. These may be great events that affect millions, or they may be individual

experiences, such as the death of a parent, a new love, or an unexpected relocation of the family.

- When comparing Boomers and Millennials, the two generations have experienced *different* significant events, both personally as well as generally. However, because the Boomer and Millennial generations overlap, there may also be certain significant societal events that both generations share as emotional touch points.

- Millennials were expected to volunteer a certain number of hours of community service. Whether willingly, this younger generation looked for ways to make the world—at least their local neighborhood—a better place in which to live. And many of these students continue to provide community service, even after the required hours have been met.

- For both generations, it seems as if they view employment as something more than simply drawing a paycheck. And both Boomers and Millennials expect work to be fulfilling on many levels—not just financial—and that includes having a sense of pride about the type of company they work for.

8

Preparing Millennials to Lead

Leaders are made, they are not born. They are made by hard effort, which is the price which all of us must pay to achieve any goal that is worthwhile.

—Vince Lombardi

Who will solve the problems of the next 50 years? International terrorism, economic challenges, worldwide food shortages, the energy crisis, and innumerable other global problems are going to confront the Millennials. Will they be uniquely qualified to succeed, or will they be doomed to fail? As we've said previously, the young men and women who comprise the Millennial group will bring many natural gifts to the challenges ahead: a global focus, a strong sense of work-life balance, technical skills, multitasking abilities, and team orientation.

But make no mistake: The future success of the Millennials will be dependent upon how they are groomed for future leadership today. They will need to be well prepared for the responsibilities, and it will be equally important to help them maintain a sense of optimism as they face tougher times ahead.

A New Profile for Learning

Few previous generations have enjoyed the educational advantages that Millennials have experienced. To be certain, the Baby Boomer generation was exposed to unprecedented levels of education following World War II. Larger numbers of Baby Boomers attended college than in any previous generation. But the Millennials began hitting the books from an earlier age and received much greater levels of structured learning.

The Millennials also grew up in a very different era. Their teachers taught them how to be managers of learning rather than passive students. They've been bombarded with information throughout their childhoods. They grew up with video games, computers, digital music, digital images, and the Internet, along with lots and lots of television.

It's safe to say that Millennials tend to be very good at learning. However, their learning style may differ a bit from their predecessors. They know how to rapidly sort through complex and sometimes massive amounts of information. They are used to thinking and reacting quickly. Their communications tend to be extremely short and to the point. One example of this is that they get their news from the Internet rather than from television or newspapers.

As a result, much is said about Millennials and their attention span. Managers and older coworkers complain that the younger generation becomes bored too quickly and loses focus. Sometimes it is exactly that, and other times it may be nothing more than fast uptake, or a combination of both.

Anyone responsible for putting together development programs—everything from initial orientation through leadership development—needs to find ways to tailor the educational design to the preferred learning style of Millennials:

- **Keep it short**—Millennials are used to receiving their information in sound bites and capsule summaries. Try to keep the information that you're delivering focused and to the point.

Don't overelaborate, and don't go off track. Once you've lost them, it may be hard to get their attention back.

▪ **Include hands-on experiences**—Although it is generally true that most adults learn better by doing rather than by listening passively, this characteristic is especially true of Millennials. Many of their teachers achieved greater learning outcomes with hands-on activities. You'll find that the more active and interactive your learning programs are, the better they will be received by your Millennials.

▪ **Design team-based learning**—Remember that this generation is used to learning in groups, as well as entertaining themselves in groups. Team-oriented learning is a great way to engage Millennials, as well as a great way to maximize the learning opportunities.

▪ **Create a visual experience**—The younger generation is used to absorbing information in highly visual forms: television, PowerPoint, Internet, cell-phone displays, and so forth. Learning materials and presentations will need to be top-notch and highly visual in order to get and keep Millennials' attention. The payoff? More rapid learning and better retention!

▪ **Make it real**—Millennials want to be able to immediately apply learning to their real world. They have little use for knowledge simply for the sake of knowledge. Make sure you connect their learning together with success in their jobs or preparation for future ones. They also want to be involved in creating their learning plan.

You can begin the process with a learning contract, ensuring shared accountability for the learning by both Millennials and their managers. This helps Millennials understand how learning directly supports success in the job and in the organization. The learning contract can also be a tool that aids manager-Millennial dialog relative to career development and support the Millennial will need from his or her boss. A sample Learning Contract follows on page 144.

Learning Contract

List the specific areas you chose for improvement.

What outcome(s) will evidence your success?

Obstacles to Success:

How You Plan to Overcome Obstacles:

Resources (including manager's support):

Anticipated Cost Savings: Revenue Gains:

_____   _____

_____   _____

(Signature)   *(Date)*

Onboarding . . . Starting Off on the Right Foot

It used to be called new-employee orientation. Nowadays, it's referred to as the onboarding process. Well-managed organizations understand that it is hypercritical to make sure new employees are appropriately welcomed, taught the ground rules, and integrated into the organization—minimally, within the first 90 days of employment. And most onboarding timetables extend beyond 90 days. What is critical is that a thoughtfully designed and well-executed process ensures that nothing and no one slips through the cracks before it's too late. This has always been true, but even more so now that the Millennial generation is entering the workforce in large numbers.

Integrating new employees from any generation into an organization is always ripe for problems. It can be bumpy for both the new hire and the veteran employees. The nightmare scenario for any organization, however, is spending large amounts of time and money to recruit the best-qualified candidates, only to have them wash out because they somehow got off on the wrong foot within the organization. So, how can that be prevented? There are many effective strategies.

We recommend that onboarding for new Millennial employees be conducted in teams as a good way to make them feel comfortable and secure. No matter how long your onboarding process is, you'll find that there are many benefits to keeping these new employees together, moving forward as a group. They're used to learning from their peers, so they will learn quicker, share insights, and problem-solve mutual dilemmas. And don't forget to include them early on in multigenerational teams across the organization. Consider communities of practice: groups who pursue learning opportunities and discussions around common areas of interest—career development, women's leadership, community volunteerism, and diversity, to name a few.

Additionally, building on the fact that Millennials seek their parents' input relative to major decisions, some organizations are inviting parents of the Millenials to onboarding programs.

Because Millennials are used to high-end technology, both in their learning environment and in their daily lives, their onboarding to a new organization should also be technological whenever possible. Use of all types of media—video, audio, computer-based, or printed—will help Millennials to learn and retain information more effectively.

Always put the Internet to work to assist their onboarding. Since one of your goals is to make your new Millennial employees feel more welcome and comfortable within the organization, you might try creating a new-employee blog, chat room, or portal as a way of putting them in touch with other new employees from their own generation. Some employers are nervous about creating independent avenues of communication among employees. No doubt there are risks, but be assured that your employees will find ways to identify other newbies. Facilitating it actually tends to make your company look pretty cool.

Another possible use of technology would be setting up virtual tours of your company. If your organization is very large and geographically spread out, this is a very cost-effective way to make new employees feel in touch with other parts of the company. Fortunately, the technology to pull this off is increasingly more cost effective, easy to use, and perhaps safer than flying employees to a remote location.

And be sure to provide your new Millennial employees with plenty of structure. This is a generation whose teachers provided detailed assignment sheets and whose "helicoptering" parents chauffeured, scheduled, and generally ran interference for them.

As you relay organizational policies and procedures in onboarding programs, remember that Millennials often don't understand the reasons behind them. Further, they'll be less inclined to take for granted that there must be a good reason, even if they don't know what it is. Be prepared to explain the "whys," along with the "whats" and "hows." It will help them become acclimated to your organization that much faster. The rule is: When in doubt, explain, explain, explain!

Consider creative ways to review organizational policies, such as true-or-false quizzes that include items like:

- T or F: The company will pay 80 percent of designated expenses for approved courses upon satisfactory completion of the courses.
- T or F: The Employee Assistance Program (EAP) is available for individuals who suffer from emotional or medical-related problems that may affect performance.
- T or F: All nonexempt-employee requests to see personnel files should be accessed through the human resources department.

You can also introduce company policies and procedures through games, patterning them after popular TV shows like *Jeopardy* or *Wheel of Fortune*.

In order to give your new-hire Millennials the broadest possible exposure to your organization, you may want to include as much cross-training and cross-department orientation as possible. New sales associates will definitely benefit from time spent in production, HR hires will benefit from exposure to field offices, and so forth. Likewise, giving your Millennial hires the opportunity to try out other positions and experience different jobs will pay big dividends down the road. Not only will cross-training and -orienting promote better understanding among new employees, but they will also build a base for future teamwork and collaboration.

It is also helpful to assign each new employee a transitional mentor to help him or her learn the ropes in a less-formal environment. The transitional mentor can be a knowledgeable veteran employee, or even a fairly new employee who has enough experience in the company to fill the role. Someone closer in age to the Millennial employee may be a better choice anyway, because he or she may better understand which particular ropes a newer employee needs to learn.

Organizational history, structure, mission, and related facts are often the focus of onboarding programs. It's actually more important to highlight corporate culture and ethics.

Corporate culture might include exposure to organizational values, expectations, traditions, legendary stories, communication patterns, work ethics, and numerous other facets of organizational life. Obviously, gossip and embarrassing tales are off limits, but covering this ground is a great way of building a bond between your new hires and the organization.

Discussing ethics, however, is another matter. Millennials are probably no different than older generations in their general sense of honor and truthfulness. But remember that they grew up in a digital age, when downloading music, movies, and software became commonplace.

A 2008 study by the Josephson Institute of Ethics found that a "substantial majority (64 percent) cheated on a test during the past year (38 percent did so two or more times), up from 60 percent and 35 percent, respectively, in 2006."[1]

Finally, a very important part of your onboarding process should be to give each new employee a picture of what a long-term career with your organization could come to mean. Some organizations even advertise career paths on their web site as a recruitment and attraction tool. Regardless, career development and progression need to be part of onboarding as well. Show them potential promotions and career paths. Help Millennials to transition from school to work and begin their development planning during their onboarding. The Transition Tool below can be used.

Transition Tool

- What knowledge or skills did you gain in school that will help you to be successful on the job?
- Based on your school experience and previous jobs, what attributes do you possess that will help you to be successful in this organization?
- What are your challenges in transitioning to a corporate environment?
- What will you do to overcome these challenges?

Millennials can discuss their transition challenges and gain advice from their mentors. It can also be helpful to bring senior leaders into the onboarding sessions to describe their career progression and to give advice to Millennials.

Rough around the Edges

You may be surprised to discover that there are some basic skills that Millennials have not yet mastered. It has been observed that quite a few Millennials show up on the first day of a job more than just a little rough around the edges. It's to your benefit to get these new hires walking, talking, and acting like professionals as soon as reasonably possible. You might offer workshops for fundamentals, such as business etiquette, writing skills, or appropriate office attire.

Let's start with business dress code. There are still some corporations that require traditional business suits, especially when employees are meeting with clients. However, many businesses today are almost completely casual when it comes to matters of dress. And for the Millennials arriving on the job in your organization, the definition of casual dress may actually be downright informal. Tank tops, flip-flops, visible tattoos, and a variety of other Millennial trademarks seem perfectly acceptable to today's younger generation and are perhaps the preferred dress in a business like a tattoo parlor. If you do not want Millennials showing up on the job dressed in this fashion, you need to be explicit with them about the standards you expect.

You may also be surprised to find that these very well-educated new employees may actually struggle with very basic communication skills. For example, letter writing in this day and age is clearly a lost art. In lieu of formal business letters, today's employees—especially younger ones—rely on e-mails, text messages, and live chat. It's not that any of these forms of communication are wrong or inappropriate. However, acceptable guidelines for style, punctuation, and grammar don't necessarily carry over from one form of communication to another. For example, the terse abbreviations that make it easier to compose a text message on the fly don't lend themselves to business documents. You may need to set aside time to talk about how your organization communicates internally, including the expected guidelines for each form of communication that is used.

Another rough spot that sometimes crops up with Millennials is the matter of manners exhibited during business lunches, dinners, and social events. It's not a particularly crucial problem most of the time, but you may find it a little surprising that some Millennials lack rudimentary social graces in this area. How to introduce yourself and others, which fork to use with what foods, and when and where to avoid alcoholic beverages are all examples of such protocol. This also encompasses knowledge about cultural differences. For instance, introductions in Japan include handing your business card (best written in Japanese) to the other person while facing them. In Holland, utensils are used in both hands and elbows are on the table. And dinners in Italy start late and seem to never end. Remember, it is a small world, after all. It might be a good idea to consider some basic-skills training and the etiquette for different company-sponsored events, especially if clients are involved.

Another possible area to consider for basic-skills training with Millennials is a matter of attitude. Things such as physically displaying impatience (foot and hand tapping, eye rolling, etc.), communicating with arrogance, and nonverbal displays of apathy are all examples of behaviors that Millennials need to eliminate, or at the very least modify.

It's a given that most Millennial employees probably don't know how they are perceived by veteran employees or senior management. Teaching them a little about company protocol could go a long way toward helping them to modify some of their more aggressive tendencies. We recommend framing this training under the rubric of organizational savvy. It's a good way to help some of your Millennials avoid potential embarrassment, if not actual career suicide.

To help them anticipate how they may react, you can also include some typically tough situations Millennials may encounter on the job. Some example scenarios you can include in your onboarding program follow:

- A senior manager is visiting your plant and stops by your cubicle to ask who you are and what you do. You respond . . .
- Your manager is not on-site very often. You are having difficulty determining priorities expected of you. You finally get a meeting with your manager to discuss expectations. You start by saying . . .
- A customer requests service beyond your level of authority. Your manager is out for the day. You . . .

- Your manager asks you to say something about yourself at the staff meeting. When you introduce yourself, you say . . .
- You suggest an option to solve a problem situation. Your manager responds, "We've never done it that way." You then respond . . .
- You become aware of a highly visible project in your area with which you would like to be involved. You approach your manager and say . . .
- You have been able to complete a lot of tasks assigned to you by your manager. However, you are unclear about the purpose and context of your assignments. You approach your manager to get a bigger picture by saying . . .
- A manager who is on the same level as your manager asks you to help out on a time-consuming project. You are worried that it will take time away from projects assigned to you by your manager. You . . .

Time Un-Management

When properly focused and motivated, your new Millennial employees will prove to be very hard workers. However, despite their previous demanding school schedules and the busy after-school routine, they may actually struggle somewhat to develop time-management skills that are necessary in a working environment. You may recall that as they progressed from grade to grade, their secretary moms and dads were very involved in helping them maintain their schedules, complete their homework, finish special projects, and get to the game on time.

In addition, you may also notice a different style of time management among your new Millennials. Baby Boomer employees were most likely taught the "A-B-C," priority-driven style of time management, typical of Alan Lakein.[2] Although Millennials are notorious for checklists galore, they actually tend to be more energy driven than time driven.

There are many Millennials who will struggle to fit their energy levels into a regimented schedule. From university days and before, many of these young people are used to pulling all-nighters, working late, sleeping late, and generally applying their energy within the parameters of their own internal clocks. Although one solution might be to offer your employees some flexibility when it comes to the timing of when they complete important projects, another is to teach them some new time-management techniques.

Ready, Camera, Action!

Whatever the training, it will need to be team-based, active, and technologically savvy.

An example of this type of action-oriented learning design is KEYGroup Quest, an interactive-learning event that helps teams to evaluate and improve their communication and problem-solving skills. In this program, participating teams receive a creative yet role-appropriate assignment, a set of clues, and a digital video camera. The team spends a day completing and videotaping the assigned tasks, employing the skills of strategy development, communication, time management, decision making, and shared accountability. At the end of the day, all the participants view highlights of the video footage to uncover each team's strengths, weaknesses, and unique interpersonal dynamics.

This type of exercise is effective because it's engaging and totally on target—the videotape doesn't lie! We've also found that this approach is especially effective with Millennials, who grew up with *Real World/Road Rules*–style videos. To them, it's the classroom meeting reality TV!

Learning to Lead

In addition to helping Millennials transition to the workplace, gain organizational savvy, manage time, and build teams, organizations need to prepare them for future leadership positions. Millennials come to the workplace with education and rich learning experiences from their youth, but they haven't always been schooled in the skills necessary to lead others.

It may be helpful for Millennials who are being groomed for leadership positions to have leadership training before being promoted to team leader or supervisory positions. The leadership training can begin with a presession survey that Millennials complete individually, as well as a section that they complete with their bosses. A sample Presession Survey follows.

Presession Survey

*Name:*_____

*Title:*_____*Phone:*_____

Complete this section individually.

1. Think of the most effective boss you ever had. What three things made him or her so effective?

2. What do you perceive to be the biggest challenges a supervisor or manager faces?

3. What would your peers (or potential direct reports) say you most need to improve or further develop?

4. How do you think a day-to-day supervisory or management job would be different than what you are currently doing?

5. In what areas would you like to gain skill or information? (Consider what is required of you in your position and review the following list of topics.)

    _____ Time and priority management, including goal setting

(continued)

_____ Delegating and holding team members accountable

_____ Coaching team members for improved performance, including motivations of different generations

_____ Communicating with team members and building trust and respect with team members

_____ Seeking input and support changes you need to make

_____ Other:

_____ Other:

_____ Other:

6. What do you believe are the three most important job duties of a supervisor or manager?

7. What does your manager indicate are your three most important supervisory or management job duties?

8. In what areas do you need to improve or further develop to be more successful as a potential supervisor or manager?

9. What does your manager indicate that you need to improve or further develop?

As mentioned previously, leadership development for Millennials should include stretch assignments for Millennials to apply learned skills. These job rotations, shadow opportunities, and special assignments provide Millennials a chance to demonstrate skills while senior managers evaluate their performance and future potential for promotion. And don't forget to provide mentors that can help guide their development.

The other way to affect hands-on, real-world learning is to provide your Millennial employees with just-in-time learning, which occurs when and where employees need it. In addition to scheduled learning sessions, employees with a specific learning need or a problem to solve can access web-based tutorials, interactive CD-ROMs, or similar tools to acquire just the information necessary to meet their learning needs or update their skills.

One advantage companies can accrue by investing in technologically-driven driven learning designs is that there are far more delivery methods today than there were in the wild and woolly frontier days of the Internet. At one time, learning participants were tied to a desktop computer at their cubicle or a video screen in a conference room in order to participate in technologically-driven training. Today, web-based learning participants can use laptops to work at the location and time of their choice. Learning can also be delivered as necessary through iPods, cell phones, and other digital devices. Learning delivery is now blended, using a variety of modes of delivery: face-to-face, webinars, online courses, avatars, distance learning, podcasts, and the like.

In the classic sense, we are really entering an era in which organizational learning and development will truly be driven by the concepts of andragogy rather than the precepts of pedagogy. Andragogy is the process of engaging adults in a structured learning experience, whereas pedagogy is the process of learning at the feet of a master teacher. Pedagogy is essentially a stand-and-deliver method, in which a passive individual simply listens and learns. The andragogy model, in contrast, is hands-on, interactive, and energizing.

For many years, learning and development experts have advocated using the andragogy model with adults because it is more effective. With Millennials now entering the workplace in large numbers, organizational-development experts are finding that it's the only model that really works consistently well. Millennials are less content to remain passive learners in their own development. They want an active role and expect to be fully engaged in the process. Their development needs to reflect this philosophy.

Mentoring—The Wind Beneath Their Wings

A particularly effective way to develop and nurture Millennials is to involve them in a mentoring program, as we mentioned earlier.

Mentors are a proven way to cultivate the careers of promising protégés through one-on-one interaction. When mentoring is effective, it's a very powerful tool to use to accelerate an employee's career. Indeed, the most successful individuals can usually point to one or more mentors who showed them the ropes, helped them overcome obstacles, and provided the kind of guidance that made a difference in their careers.

One reason this is an effective strategy for developing Millennials is that they grew up responding to role models. Unlike previous generations, most of these young people have enjoyed unusually close relationships with their parents, with whom Millennials have come to view as role models. Teachers have also frequently served as a source of inspiration to them.

And let's not forget the tales of heroism that emerged from terrorist attacks. In the hours, days, and months following the tragic events of 9/11, the London bombings of 2005, the 2004 train bombings in Spain, and the Tokyo gas attacks of 1995, people around the world heard tales of hundreds of heroes who risked life and limb to secure the safety of others.

Millennials are very willing to place their trust in and listen to advice from people they respect. The one-on-one interaction between a mentor and a protégé makes them feel special and reinforces their self-confidence. A typical mentoring program is designed to match senior executives and midlevel managers with up-and-coming young people within the organization. The only caveat is to make sure that you match mentors and protégés appropriately. Make sure the goals of the interactions are clear to both parties, and be sure to set any limits or parameters that may be required. Mentoring programs usually include the organization's mentoring vision or mission statement, both formal and informal relationships, and an employee-driven process (e.g., a task force that manages and communicates process). Potential mentors may be identified in the organization, and the organization often devotes a portal on the company intranet in order to highlight those who have volunteered to mentor others, including a short biography and areas in which they may best provide guidance. Mentors should possess the following core skills:

- Listening empathetically
- Questioning, using both open- and close-ended questions
- Giving candid, diplomatic feedback
- Providing both encouragement and challenge

Millennials who are potential mentees need to assess their skill levels, interest areas, career goals, knowledge about the organization, and personal-development goals. Consider providing Millennials with some thought starters that they can use in discussions with their mentor(s):

- I feel proud about my ability to . . .
- I know that I will need to watch . . .
- I am looking forward to . . .
- I will be cautious about . . .
- What I want my coworkers to understand about me is . . .
- In my career, I want to . . .

In some cases, it might be appropriate to educate Millennials about the protocols of interacting with senior management. As we said earlier, such guidance could come as early as the onboarding process or in business-etiquette-type programs. It may not be a safe assumption that Millennials understand when and where it would be appropriate to initiate contact and what is or isn't open for discussion. Millennials tend to take matters of privacy and privilege for granted. They will often willingly share information that older generations may find to be too personal. But simply make the rules clear, and you'll have fewer problems.

Additionally, mentoring programs usually include workshops for mentors and mentees and organizational tools to help them to get started, to guide their relationship, and to evaluate both the relationship and the results.

The Future of Management

Of the questions we are most often asked by our clients, the most common is, "What kind of leaders will Millennials make some day?" Well, we don't have a foolproof crystal ball for peering into the future. But it seems to be a cinch that we can expect Millennials to naturally bring a global viewpoint to the workplace.

Remember that the Millennials have grown up in a far flatter world than the one their Boomer parents inherited. The globalization of the world economy has altered how we think about markets, supply chains, and competition. The widespread adoption of the World Wide Web has given Millennials tremendous power and a global perspective.

And at the end of the day, when thinking about the future of Millennial leadership, it only seems natural to expect that they will fully deploy the technological tools at their fingertips. Millennials are a generation of supergeeks in some ways, and they will truly use technology to make work simpler, more productive, and less burdensome.

In speaking on the global impact of the Internet, Thomas L. Friedman said, "It created a global platform that allowed more people to plug and play, collaborate and compete, share knowledge and share work, than anything we have ever seen in the history of the world."[3]

Most organizations today are far flatter, with fewer managers and far fewer levels of hierarchy. Also remember that Millennials were trained to challenge their teachers and to work closely with teachers, parents, and coaches in a more collegial atmosphere than the previous generation ever imagined. We can expect Millennial leaders to collaborate in the workplace.

This generation has grown up hearing, "Collaborate, collaborate, collaborate!" Teamwork and teambuilding won't merely be lip service to Millennials as they take command of the ship. Their slogan might well become, "Collaborate or fail!"

Millennial leaders will take individual differences, not only as a matter of course, but also as a matter of organizational strength. We can expect them to employ differing strengths for the benefit of the team and the organization. The notion of merely tolerating such differences will simply be foreign to them. Millennials are already a mobile generation, so it only seems natural to expect them to leverage vastly differing work styles, whether in the office, at home, in the car, on vacation, or anywhere else people choose to work.

Armed with a perspective like that, one can only imagine what the future of the workplace will be under the direction of Millennial leaders!

Keys to Chapter 8

- The future success of the Millennials will be dependent upon how they are groomed for future leadership today. They will need to be well prepared for the responsibilities, and it will be equally important to help them maintain a sense of optimism as they face tougher times ahead.
- Millennials' learning style may differ a bit from their predecessors. They know how to rapidly sort through complex and sometimes massive amounts of information. They are used to thinking and reacting quickly. Their communications tend to be extremely short and to the point.
- Anyone responsible for putting together development programs—everything from initial orientation through leadership development—needs to find ways to tailor the educational design to the preferred learning style of Millennials: short, hands-on, team based, visual, and real to life.
- Because Millennials are used to high-end technology, both in their learning environment and in their daily lives, their onboarding to a new organization should also be technological whenever possible. Use of all types of media—video, audio,

computer-based, or printed—will help Millennials to learn and retain information more effectively.

- Provide your new Millennial employees with plenty of structure. This is a generation whose teachers provided detailed assignment sheets and whose "helicoptering" parents chauffeured, scheduled, and generally ran interference for them.

- Give your new Millennials the broadest possible exposure to your organization. You may want to include as much cross-training and cross-department orientation as possible.

- Assign each new employee a transitional mentor to help him or her learn the ropes in a less-formal environment. The transitional mentor can be a knowledgeable veteran employee, or even a fairly new employee, who has enough experience in the company to fill the role.

- Include learning about corporate culture in your onboarding programs. This includes exposure to organizational values, expectations, traditions, legendary stories, communication patterns, work ethics, and numerous other facets of organizational life.

- Ethics discussions are also important to have with newly hired Millennials.

- Millennials may struggle somewhat to develop time-management skills that are necessary in a working environment. They often display a different style of time management, in contrast to the Baby Boomer employees, who are most likely taught the "A-B-C," priority-driven style of time management. Millennials actually tend to be more energy-driven than time-driven.

- It may be helpful for Millennials who are being groomed for leadership positions to have leadership-development training before being promoted to team leader or supervisory positions.

- A particularly effective way to develop and nurture Millennials is to involve them in a mentoring program. Mentors are a proven way to cultivate the careers of promising protégés through one-on-one interaction. When mentoring is effective, it's a very powerful tool to use to accelerate an employee's career.

9

R U Communicating with Millennials?

The single biggest problem in communication is the illusion that it has taken place.

—Gandhi

Effective communication is problematic under almost any circumstance, but combine the usual difficulties in communication with the problem of trying to communicate across generations, and you have a real challenge. Anytime you have a younger generation beginning to enter the workplace in large numbers, as is the case today with Millennials, there are bound to be some conflicts. The new generation typically seeks to differentiate itself from the older generation, so you have inevitable differences in interests, music, dress, and language.

Psychologists could probably give you a pretty detailed explanation of why young people always seem to rebel against older people. Obviously, there is a very strong desire among youth for independence and a deep-seated need not to appear to be clones of their parents. But generational differences are also caused by the varied environments in which people were raised.

Certainly, the Baby Boomers grew up in circumstances that many of their parents consider being in the lap of luxury. Likewise, when

163

Baby Boomers look at the circumstances in which their children grew up, they are both a little incredulous and probably more than a little envious.

Nowhere is the difference between two generations more apparent than in how each of those generations uses language. The Millennials, like their Boomer parents before them, communicate with each other using a rich mixture of slang language, colloquialisms, technical jargon, and chat speak. At times, Millennials can appear to be speaking a truly foreign language to their older coworkers and bosses. And to be sure, the differences in communication style from generation to generation—including Matures, Boomers, Generation X, and Millennials—may sometimes appear to be an insurmountable gulf.

However, it is important for anyone working in a multigenerational environment to consider how the communication style of certain coworkers can provide important insights into another generation's thought processes, perceptions, and values.

The English writer Robert Louis Stevenson pointed out that "man is a creature who lives not upon bread alone, but primarily by catchwords." Samuel Johnson, an earlier writer who was also an Englishman, said, "Language is the dress of thought."

Both of these writers understood that our use of language on a daily basis, even the use of casual or informal language, helped human beings to better understand their own world. Through the use of our daily language, we relate to the world around us, as well as to each other. So, by understanding the way other generations communicate, each generation becomes better able to bridge any experience gaps or to leap any chasms of understanding.

The KEYGroup Youth Culture Quiz

For the past several years, we have both been invited to speak to the leaders and staff of numerous organizations on the subject of managing across generational differences. Usually when we give these presentations, we find ourselves speaking to heterogeneous groups, composed of members from two, three, and sometimes even four different generational groups.

Sometimes, it can be hard to demonstrate how sharp some of the differences among generations can be. One of the methods that we found to be very useful in illustrating how the Millennial generation differs from its predecessors is the administration of a quiz we developed. In addition, we have placed this quiz on our web site, where it's been viewed and completed thousands of times.

We have found that one's ability to correctly answer the questions on the quiz is a pretty good indicator of which generation he or she belongs to. More importantly, those who struggle with some of the definitions and meanings usually find it eye-opening to receive a glimpse into the minds of most Millennials.

Try your hand at answering our youth-culture trivia quiz. The correct answers follow the quiz.

KEYGroup Youth Culture Trivia Quiz

1. Under current young-lingo standards, which of the following uses of the word "mad" fits most appropriately?

(a) I'm going to make this dance mad!

(b) That teacher lectured for mad long!

(c) Did you see him mad out on that piñata?

2. When someone says "fives," he or she is:

(a) attempting to solicit a slapping high five from a buddy.

(b) telling friends that he or she is planning to leave in 5 minutes.

(c) claiming a recently vacated seat, with intent to reclaim it in the near future.

3. Of the following slang terms and given meanings, pick the pair that has no relationship:

(a) "Busted"—Muscular
(b) "Whip"—Vehicle
(c) "Bag"—Acquired
(d) "Bling"—Jewelry

4. "Shotty no blitz" means:

(a) making a mistake, but one that is correctable.
(b) getting blindsided by a good friend.
(c) calling the front seat, without the chance of someone else claiming it.

5. Of the following slang terms and given meanings, pick the pair that has no relationship:

(a) "Paper"—Money
(b) "Dis"—Insult
(c) "Rolled"—Exhausted
(d) "Fresh"—Extremely nice, superior quality

6. Of the following slang terms and given meanings, pick the pair that has no relationship:

(a) "Nappy"—Gross, disgusting
(b) "Peeps"—People
(c) "One"—Dollar bill

7. What is the nickname for the Michigan freshmen basketball class of 1992, who took the school to the Final Four and changed the style of shorts in basketball from short and tight to long and baggy?

_____

8. Of the following slang terms and given meanings, pick the pair that has no relationship:

(a) "Cheddar"—Awesome
(b) "Gravy"—Easy
(c) "Sick"—Cool
(d) "Skeez"—Sleazy person

9. Match the following 1960s terms with their current-lingo synonyms:

(a) Pig out	(1) Bounce
(b) Right on	(2) PoPo
(c) Pad	(3) Amped
(d) Beat feet	(4) Monster
(e) Jazzed	(5) Crib
(f) Fuzz	(6) Word

The Youth Culture Trivia Quiz—Answers

1. Under current young-lingo standards, which of the following uses of the word "mad" fits most appropriately?

(b) **That teacher lectured for mad long!**

2. When someone says "fives," he or she is:

(c) **claiming a recently vacated seat, with intent to reclaim it in the near future.**

3. Of the following slang terms and given meanings, pick the pair that has no relationship:

(a) **"Busted"—Muscular**

4. "Shotty no blitz" means:

   (c) calling the front seat, without the chance of someone else claiming it.

5. Of the following slang terms and given meanings, pick the pair that has no relationship:

   (c) "Rolled"—Exhausted

6. Of the following slang terms and given meanings, pick the pair that has no relationship:

   (c) "One"—Dollar bill

7. What is the nickname for the Michigan freshmen basketball class of 1992 who took the school to the Final Four and changed the style of shorts in basketball from short and tight to long and baggy?

   the Fab Five

8. Of the following slang terms and given meanings, pick the pair that has no relationship:

   (a) "Cheddar"—Awesome

9. Match the following 1960s terms with their current-lingo synonyms:

   (a)—(4), (b)—(6), (c)—(5), (d)—(1), (e)—(3), (f)—(2)

Hopefully, you learned a little bit about some slang phrases and colloquial terms that are popular among Millennials. However, for a more thorough look into the way that they communicate, continue reading.

Don't Forget about "Boomerisms"

It's very important for readers who belong to the Baby Boom generation to remember that the slang language they used was as bedeviling to parents then as their own children's slang language is to them now. It goes without saying that the hip terms of the early 1960s were just as fresh and original and vivid as the slang language of today. However, when we look back, many of the terms that confused our parents seem like normal language today.

However, for members of Generation X and the Millennials, it might prove useful to take a look at some of the fashionable terms that formed the unique vocabulary of the period. If you grew up in America during the 1960s:

- Something fun was a "gas."
- To "dig" something was to understand or like it.
- Something "far out" was excellent or cool.
- If you called something "groovy," it meant you thought it was cool.
- The police were called "fuzz" (along with several less attractive terms).
- To "rap" meant to talk (but not in the musical sense).
- Saying "lay it on me" meant "tell me" or "speak your piece."
- Something "hairy" was dangerous or out of control.
- Clothes were "threads" or "rags."

This sampling of 1960s slang language applies primarily to American English. Although, through the pervasive spread of American culture around the world—especially throughout English-speaking countries—it's possible that most middle-aged speakers of English will recognize many of the terms.

The Language of "X-istentialism"

Often lost amid discussions of the multigenerational workforce is Generation X. Born between 1965 and 1979, Generation X was the offspring of the very oldest Boomers. They've been given many different terms by writers over the years, including the "13ᵗʰ generation," the "Slacker generation," and the "Grunge generation." We discussed Generation X in much more detail in Chapter 4. Now we need to consider some of the unique language and terminology of Gen Xers, as well as the terminology of Boomers and Millennials.

The members of Generation X began entering the workforce in the mid to late 1980s, a period of rapid growth in technology. Therefore, like the Millennials, much of their communication style centers around technical jargon. They are also noted for a certain amount of cynicism and negativity about their role in the workplace, thus accounting for some particularly vivid terminology.

In 1990, novelist Douglas Coupland wrote about some of the unique characteristics of this first group. His book *Generation X: Tales for an Accelerated Culture*, published in 1990, was one of the first to describe the angst of a generation that saw itself doomed to a career of unfulfilling, low-paying positions. He coined the phrase "McJobs" to describe the type of positions that Gen Xers were likely to have. Addressing other characteristics of the generation, he mentioned "likeness," which he describes as their diminishing expectations of material wealth; "101-ism," which is the tendency to pick apart all aspects of life using barely understood pop psychology as a tool; and "option paralysis," which means that, given unlimited options, Gen X took none.[1]

Similarly, members of Generation X were also prone to coin imaginative catchphrases to describe the culture of the workplace in which they labored. Much of their terminology revolved around technology, as did the terminology of the next generation down the pike. However, some of the workplace nomenclature of this generation shows a very strong sense of irony, if not a dark sense of humor:

- Googling your own name is called "ego surfing" by Generation X (www.dictionary.com)
- Someone who enjoys stressful situations but manages to whine about them is referred to as a "stress puppy." (www.main.edu/~zubrick/genxjar.html)
- In every organization, there are a handful of people whose creativity is unbridled. Gen Xers call these folks "idea hamsters."
- To previous generations, a sitcom was a television show. To Gen Xers, "SITCOM" stands for "single income, two children, oppressive mortgage," a condition most wish to avoid.
- The "Elvis Year" for the Cabbage Patch Kids was 1983. It was the year the Cabbage Patch Kid mania reached the peak of its popularity. (www.main.edu/~zubrick/genxjar.html)
- If you make personal copies at work, you have a "Xerox subsidy." (www.main.edu/~zubrick/genxjar.html)

If there is an underlying current of cynicism behind some of the phrases coined by members of Generation X, it can also be seen that there is a healthy sense of humor and a willingness to see the ironies and inconsistencies of modern office life.

The Influence of the Sound Bite

One thing that differentiates the era in which Millennials grew up from the era in which Boomers grew up was the prevalence of the sound bite. By definition, a "sound bite" is a short phrase or expression that is vivid and easily remembered, particularly for consumption by the media. The sound bite has become such a prevalent concept that it has actually become a distinguishing characteristic of the way young people communicate.

We first began hearing the term *sound bite* bandied around during the administration of Ronald Reagan. Reagan was famous for his ability to use short, pithy phrases that seem to sum up more complex ideas. For example, he once threatened to veto pending legislation by daring Congress with the catchphrase, "Go ahead, make my day"—an actual phrase from the Clint Eastwood film *Dirty Harry*.

He admonished Soviet-leader Gorbachev to loosen the country's control of Eastern Europe with the phrase, "Mr. Gorbachev, tear down this wall." Ronald Reagan, who is generally known to be a master of the media, understood that television and newspaper editors needed to cram as much information as possible into as short a space as they have available. In order to assure that his or her point would be represented on the evening news, a politician had to be able to craft a short, memorable line.

Combine that with the avalanche of advertising slogans that we are bombarded with through radio, television, and print media, and it is easy to understand why we respond more readily to short, well-crafted expressions. It seems as though we no longer prefer to think in more depth when we can substitute a quick and dirty conclusion or slogan for a thorough analysis.

When we look at how the Millennial generation communicates, we have to consider the extent to which their concept of communication—of expressing complex ideas, at least—is influenced by the notion of the sound bite. With Millennials, it can safely be said that less is more when it comes to communication. Succinct messages delivered in a timely fashion are what Millennials often seem to prefer. The only difficulty is that members of all generations may not always understand the context or shorthand of a Millennial's message.

The Millennial Communication Mindset

If it can be safely said that Generation X was raised with new technologies, it must be noted that Millennials were totally immersed in the technologies of their era. For Gen Xers, technology was a brave new world. For Millennials, technology was the world. So, it is safe to say that to the Millennial mind, the vernacular of their generation is almost totally defined in one form or another by communication technologies: cell phones, computers, text messaging, the Internet, digital audio, and voice mail. To this generation, the BlackBerry is way more than a fruit. And the iPhone—don't even get them started!

Sometimes we refer to the Millennials as the "Wired generation," but this is probably an inaccurate perception. If anything, these young people are truly the "wireless generation." The Boomers and Gen Xers before them, while enjoying the fruits of electronic communication, were nonetheless tethered to their offices, family rooms, or vehicles. Early cell phones were monstrous and hardwired to power sources. Notebook computers are a relatively recent phenomenon (although lap-crushing portable computers have been around for years). Early adopters of the Internet were almost certainly always homebound or work bound, since they required a hardwired telephone line.

The technologies that most Millennials have grown up with are increasingly smaller, truly portable, and almost completely untethered. The vision of being able to connect via e-mail and Internet (or instant messaging) from almost anywhere has become a commonplace reality, at least for the younger generation. Their penchant for communicating with their friends on a 24-7 basis from almost anywhere—home, work, church, shopping, sports events, darkened movie theaters, and similar places—has made them the most connected generation ever.

By the same token, the duration and depth of the messages they exchange with friends (on a seemingly continuous basis) appears to be very minimal. Instant messaging, for example, doesn't lend itself to lengthy diatribes. Even the purpose of one of the newest Internet fads, Twitter, seems to be rather pointless. Twitter is a web site that merely allows young people to exchange extremely simple messages describing the activity and place they happen to be in at that precise moment. The messages are usually not very meaningful and include answers to questions like "what are you doing right now?" or "where are you?"

Millennial Speak

When it comes to describing the ways in which Millennials differ from their predecessors, you have to consider that a lot of their communication is technology-driven. That means that they have had to adapt to the requirements of their communication technologies, such as instant messaging. But it also means that they have grown up in an environment in which technology has flavored the forms of communication.

A significant number of the new words that have entered the English language over the past 25 years have been born of technical jargon. Computer programmers are a creative lot when it comes to coining new terms or phrases, and many of those terms have spilled over into everyday life. Consider the following examples of freshly minted Millennial terms:

- **Compunicate**—This refers to the art of conducting a conversation with a coworker or friend using text messaging or instant messaging while you are both in the same room. (www.urbandictionary.com)
- **Defriend**—Whenever you remove someone from your address book or your list of contacts, you have "de-friended" them. (www.unwords.com)
- **Lifestreaming**—This is the online posting (blog) of an individual's daily activities in minute detail. (www.wordspy.com)
- **Moofer**—In this age of portable computers and cell phones, many individuals take advantage of these "mobile out-of-office" technologies, making them "moofers." (www.double-tongued.com)
- **Porntastic**—This is an adjective that refers to something so good it is considered somewhat sexy. (www.urbandictionary.com)

Part of the fascination we have with slang language and colloquialisms is that they are fresh and fashionable. There is no better way to demonstrate that you are "in" than by peppering your speech with current and popular slang expressions. Conversely, there is no faster way to show that you are a "poser" (slang for phony) than by using language that is now considered passé.

All language is a bit of a moving target; particularly slang language. We run the risk of providing the reader with current popular expressions that in only a few years may seem dated and out of touch. Bear this in mind when you're trying to bridge the communication gap between generations, as the language of any given generation is in a constant state of flux.

Two Thumbs Up . . . and Down

It can truly be said that we are now living in a global cell-phone culture. By 2003, there were about 1.16 billion subscriptions to mobile-telephone services worldwide—indeed, more people had mobile subscriptions than subscriptions to traditional land lines. The number of mobile subscribers worldwide recently reached 2 billion. With the earth's population at 6.6 billion people, this means that roughly 3 out of every 10 people now have mobile devices. Connecting the first billion mobile users took 12 years; connecting the second billion took 2.5 years; and connecting the third billion will take less than that.[2]

The true communication possibilities of mobile phones may have yet to be fully explored by Gen Xers and Baby Boomers. Members of both of those generations tend to prefer voice mail and e-mail communications, while ignoring the other communication possibilities of their electronic umbilical cords.

To most members of the Baby Boom generation, the introduction of e-mail was a revelation. The idea that one could communicate with fellow employees no matter where in the world they were located, almost instantly, seemed truly revolutionary. And without question, e-mail certainly has revolutionized the way organizations operate today.

However, the key word in this gee-whiz technology is the word "almost." E-mail is speedy and nearly instantaneous, but the protocol doesn't demand that one knows the e-mail was either delivered or read the very second it was transmitted.

In contrast, the communication technologies that drive the Millennial generation are instant messaging and text messaging.

Instant messaging was an Internet-based phenomenon that took off in the mid-1990s with the introduction of a program called ICQ (code for "I seek you"). Even more popular was AOL Instant Messenger (AIM), a program introduced by network service provider America Online. Both of these programs allowed two or more users to engage in a chat with each other, exchanging questions, comments, and responses instantaneously. It was literally akin to having a typed phone conversation. There was no transmitting an e-mail and waiting for a reply, which may or may not arise immediately.

Of course, one drawback to instant messaging was the fact that not everyone had a computer, had access to a computer, or was in a place where computers were readily available. Enter text messaging.

In the same time period—the mid-1990s—cell-phone manufacturers began adding a service to their equipment that allowed cell-phone users to communicate with each other instantly, similar to instant messaging. From that humble beginning, short message service (SMS) is now the most widely used mobile-data service in the world. A Mobinet study found that 56 percent of multimedia mobile-phone users said they use their phones to access the Internet or check e-mail at least once a month—a significant jump from the 36 percent who said they did so in the 2004 Mobinet study. Thirty-five percent of all mobile-phone users around the globe use mobile-data service regularly.[3] It's safe to say that once again, the appeal of real-time instantaneous communications is what attracts users to text messaging. That and the fact that while they may not always have a computer available, almost everyone, including a substantial number of Millennials, always seem to have a cell phone handy.

The significance of this technology is that it tends to drive many of the communication patterns of the younger generation. Baby Boomers have been slower to adopt this technology for daily use but are motivated to do so to stay in touch with their kids.

But text messaging has become so pervasive that it is beginning to creep into advertising, earning the nickname "textvertising."

For example, several years ago Frito-Lay began displaying billboards with nothing more than the cryptic message "inNw?" on the signage. The campaign was intended to promote a new flavor of Doritos corn chips to young Americans. The intentional use of text-message-like slogans was particularly targeted at Millennial snackers, who were directed to Frito-Lay's web site for more information. Once there, visitors were informed that "inNw?" stands for "if not now, when?" Site visitors were also encouraged to join in a text-message-based dialog ("Speak UR Mind") and to "Vote 4 UR Fave Music Videos."

Frito-Lay's strategy marked the first time that instant messaging was the core concept behind a large marketing campaign. But Frito-Lay isn't the only marketer using text messaging to sell its products.

In a series of ads for AT&T mobile service, the mother of the family is shown complaining to her two children about the number of minutes they have been burning up by texting their friends. Naturally, the children answer their mother in "text speak." But as they are arguing, Grandma is sitting in a corner of the room, rapidly punching the dial pad on her cell phone. When the mother asks Grandma, "Mom, who could you be texting?" the elderly lady replies, "My BFF Marge" (which translated means "my best friend forever Marge").

It is the image of the family's grandmother—undoubtedly a member of the Mature generation—adapting so readily to an instant-message communication medium that represents a sort of ideal market for cell-phone providers—to sell SMS to everyone in the family and not just the Millennial offspring.

Consider the example that follows.

Texting It Like It Is

Communicating with your Millennials doesn't have to be a problem. It's just a matter of understanding the lingo. Between texting each other over their phones and instant messaging on their computers, Millennials have developed a unique language.

IDK, you might think they should just GAL and communicate like everyone else. But Millennials would tell you DHYB. How they talk with one another is NOYB. But AFAIC, it helps to be on the same wavelength, even though many Boomers consider it TMI.

AAMOF, it's not just a hobby with Millennials. They're AATK, whether it's a smart phone or a laptop, so texting is just ADAD to them. Sometimes it's work related, but sometimes it's a case of AWLTP. And if they get caught, it could prove to be a CLM. It might even be CS!

I mean, CMIW, but most employers take a dim view of goofing off on the job, whether it's surfing the net at their desk or IMing from the break room. My advice to younger workers is to MYL and lay off the shorthand. B4YKI, the boss may catch on to the acronyms and YBS.

GGN . . . one of my children is texting me.

Glossary

AAMOF:	as a matter of fact
AATK:	always at the keyboard
ADAD:	another day, another dollar
AFAIC:	as far as I'm concerned
AWLTP:	avoiding work like the plague
B4YKI:	before you know it
CLM:	career-limiting move
CMIW:	correct me if I'm wrong
CS:	career suicide
DHYB:	don't hold your breath

GAL:	get a life
GGN:	gotta go now
IDK:	I don't know
IM:	instant message
MYL:	mind your language
NOYB:	none of your business
TMI:	too much information
YBS:	you'll be sorry

Tips for Communicating with Millennials

While it's useful to understand the communication patterns of the younger generation, it isn't necessary for Baby Boomer and Generation X coworkers to assume the same patterns themselves. In other words, you won't need to sound like Grandma in the AT&T commercials in order to get your message across. What is necessary, however, is to maintain some flexibility in the degree of patience. What may seem like poor communication or bad behavior on the part of your Millennial employees and coworkers may simply be normal patterns for them.

For example, if it is considered unacceptable in your company for employees to text message during meetings, you may need to make this clear to your younger employees. Most companies don't permit employees to take cell-phone calls during meetings, and there is no reason to break that same rule with SMS. Just don't assume that Millennials will see texting as inappropriate.

Don't over-rely on snail mail (letters or interoffice memos) for critical communications. Remember, Millennials in particular tend to be real-time oriented and may not respond to "tree-killer" communication forms. Don't expect instant replies to all e-mails (that's what in-baskets are for), and don't be surprised to receive a callback from a Millennial who didn't bother to listen to the lengthy voice mail message you left. Millennials prefer direct instant communications.

The same also holds true for face-to-face contact. Millennials prefer direct one-to-one communication to large group discussions. Remember that they are used to receiving lots of direct feedback from teachers and parents, so they will be expecting the same type of interactions and access with their bosses.

Another thing to remember is that Millennials are extreme multitaskers. They think nothing of writing a paper, listening to music, and texting one of their friends all at the same time, accompanied by a television blaring in the background. The drawback to this blend of split attention for those trying to communicate with Millennials is that important messages may become lost in the noise. If you have a critical message to deliver to Millennials, you may want to send it via their preferred mode.

If the matter is truly important—a crucial deadline, changing strategies, new requirements, or unexpected problems—it's worth taking the extra time to send an e-mail, write a memo, text a message (if your thumbs are up to it), or say it in person. Better safe than sorry.

Key Words to Communicate with Millennials

If you are a leader charged with managing Millennials, you want to make sure that above all else, you maintain a positive communication environment. Millennials are used to receiving a great deal of positive reinforcement. They expect it, and they respond well to positive communications. The following are some suggestions for making sure your interactions stay focused and positive.

All successful leaders put language to work, even though no two leaders are exactly alike. Some leaders have great technical knowledge, while others have great vision. Some are charismatic and inspirational, while others are introspective and insightful. But no matter what gifts they bring to the role of leader, they all have one thing in common: Their primary tools of leadership are words.

Leaders use language to inform, inspire, and persuade. Whether through speeches, vision statements, or annual reports, a leader has to find the right words to connect employees and managers with each other, as well as with other stakeholders.

And when you're trying to understand organizational culture, words are critical! The way people talk about their work, how they describe their customers, the job titles they use, and how they speak with coworkers all help to define the culture.

But sometimes you have to listen very carefully to catch a sense of the organization's culture. Slogans, posters, and marketing campaigns, which are highly visible in some organizations, may not reflect the *true* culture. It's what their leaders and employees say that really defines a winning culture.

Language can be tricky, as Mark Twain observed. How often do we choose the wrong word or use a term out of context, only to have it blow up in our faces? And if you're an organizational leader, you have to be very sensitive to how your language impacts others. Do you use language that clarifies, motivates, and inspires? Or does your language tend to confuse, discourage, or demoralize?

Effective leaders use language that makes employees feel valued, encouraged, and respected. When communicating with individuals or groups, try to use language that reflects these needs:

- **Words of Inclusion:** Millennials, like most employees, feel a greater sense of loyalty when you use terms like "team" and "partner" and talk about "our" goals and customers. Successful companies like to refer to employees using terms like "associates," "colleagues," and "teammates." When you talk about "subordinates" and "workers," you tend to create an us-versus-them mentality.

- **Words of Empowerment:** In order to empower people, you have to express confidence in their abilities to get the job done ("I know you can do it" and "you're the best person for the task"). At all costs, try to avoid undermining Millennials with expressions of doubt, such as "I'll give you a chance," or "nobody else wanted to do it." Instead of giving employees "deadlines" and "due dates," try to give them "goals" and "targets."

- **Words of Success:** Thriving organizations have a vocabulary of success; they use words that help employees understand what needs to be accomplished. People in winning organizations tend to use terms like "victory," "achievement," "result," "outcome," "performance," and "payoff." In struggling organizations, you're more likely to hear people talking about "coming up short," "botching a job," "dropping the ball," and similar phrases. The language of success is energizing, while the language of failure is demoralizing.

But actions also speak as loudly as words. In these demanding times, the best way leaders can ensure a dynamic, adaptable workplace is to encourage positive communication patterns. Whenever we visit an organization for the first time, we like to wander around, listen, and observe the types of language being employed in speeches, memos, conversations, signs, and other communications. It usually doesn't take long to tell whether the culture is energized and positive or stagnant and negative.

But building a positive, productive working environment requires more than words alone. Your behaviors and actions have to match your words as well, because employees need to believe that their leaders really care about *them* as much as they care about the bottom line.

In the meantime, try to become more aware of how you and your leaders use language to communicate with employees. Are you setting a positive, encouraging tone, or are you fostering a negative climate? As Goethe said, "Correction does much, but encouragement does more."

Communication within any organization has to be designed to set a tone of focus, enthusiasm, success, and fulfillment. It isn't only Millennials who respond well to a positive-communication climate. All employees prefer to be praised rather than criticized. All employees prefer to be appreciated rather than ignored. All employees prefer to contribute to the success of the team rather than to be blamed for other people's failures.

It's possible that the upbringing of the Baby Boomer generation and the upbringing of Generation X may have in some ways contributed to the willingness of many employees to accept a negative work environment. This is not to say that Boomers and Xers prefer negativity, but only that they grew up with more of it than the Millennials and thus may be more accepting of it.

When we look back 50 years from now to that period in which members of the Millennial generation began entering the workforce in large numbers, we may actually begin to see the start of a new era. Millennials may well set a new standard for creating a positive, productive, and motivating work environment that features positive communications and ample positive reinforcement. After all, most of them grew up in that type of household, so why would they expect anything less at work?

Keys to Chapter 9

- Nowhere is the difference between two generations more apparent than in how each of those generations uses language. The Millennials, like their Boomer parents before them, communicate with each other using a rich mixture of slang language, colloquialisms, technical jargon, and chat speak.
- Anyone working in a multigenerational environment should consider how the communication style of certain coworkers can provide important insights into another generation's thought processes, perceptions, and values.

- One thing that differentiates the era in which Millennials grew up from the era in which Boomers grew up was the prevalence of the sound bite. A "sound bite" is a short phrase or expression that is vivid and easily remembered, particularly for consumption by the media. The sound bite has become such a prevalent concept that it has actually become a distinguishing characteristic of the way young people communicate.
- Succinct messages delivered in a timely fashion are what Millennials often seem to prefer. The only difficulty is that members of other generations may not understand the context or shorthand of a Millennial's message.
- For Millennials, the vernacular of their generation is almost totally defined in one form or another by communication technologies: cell phones, computers, text messaging, the Internet, digital audio, and voice mail.
- The Millennials' penchant for communicating with their friends on a 24-7 basis from almost anywhere—home, work, church, shopping, sports events, darkened movie theaters, and similar places—has made them the most connected generation ever.
- Millennials have grown up in an environment in which technology has flavored the forms of communication. A significant number of the new words that have entered the English language over the past 25 years have been born of technical jargon.
- Mobile-phone users around the globe use mobile-data service regularly. It's safe to say that once again, the appeal of real-time instantaneous communications is what attracts users to text messaging.
- Don't over-rely on snail mail (letters or interoffice memos) for critical communications. Remember, Millennials in particular tend to be real time-oriented and may not respond to "tree-killer" communication forms.

- Another thing to remember is that Millennials are extreme multitaskers. If you have a critical message to deliver to a Millennial coworker or employee, you may want to maximize that message by delivering it using the medium of his or her choice.
- Learn to use language to inform, inspire, and persuade. Whether through speeches, vision statements, or annual reports, a leader has to find the right words to connect employees and managers with each other, as well as with other stakeholders.

10

Marketing to Millennials

Make it simple. Make it memorable. Make it inviting to look at. Make it fun to read.

—Leo Burnett

The population size and sales potential of the Millennial generation hasn't been lost on marketers. They've had their eye on them since they were teenagers in the 1990s. Because the purpose of our book is to look at Millennials from the perspective of employers, it may not seem logical to include a chapter on marketing to Millennials. However, in one very important respect, many organizations ought to be interested in marketing themselves to Millennial job candidates in order to reach and recruit the best employment prospects.

Modern recruiting is as much about marketing as it is about talent management. Unless you can position your organization to young job candidates as an ideal place in which to develop a career, you run the risk of losing millions of dollars in turnover and lost opportunities.

Underestimating the Millennial Market

When brand names first began targeting their advertising to Millennials in the early 1990s, they automatically assumed the same marketing that had appealed to Generation X and Baby Boomers would still be relevant. Their assumption was that a snappy slogan combined with attractive visuals would be sufficient to gain the attention—and ultimately the dollars—of young people. However, a series of missteps by very powerful brand names served to prove that the Millennial market was not going to be the same as the markets that had preceded it.

Perhaps no brand has been more powerful than Nike. With their history of innovative footwear and one of the most highly visible logos in the world, Nike seemed to be in a very strong position to win the hearts and minds of Millennial teenagers back in the 1990s. As cited by *BusinessWeek,* the company's slick advertising that featured celebrities fell flat when the company was rocked by some negative press regarding working conditions and Olympic sponsorship.

The *BusinessWeek* article also highlighted Levi's, another iconic brand, which also discovered that the Millennial generation is somewhat resistant to high-profile marketing campaigns. The wake-up call occurred for Levi's in 1997, when it discovered its market share was sliding amongst members of the Millennial generation. The company's product line had become stale, and the marketing continued to rely on the same strategies and media that previously had appealed to Baby Boomers and Generation X. To avoid further market-share erosion, Levi's was forced to reinvent its product lines with designs more appealing to teenagers and to restructure its marketing to appeal specifically to Millennials. Included in their efforts were more effective use of web-based marketing and greater use of teenage focus groups to track trends.[1]

Erroneous marketing assumptions and misdirected advertising campaigns taught many marketers several important lessons about what it takes to advertise to Millennials. But one lesson seems clear: Millennials are one tough group to market to. They grew up immersed in all sorts of media—print, radio, television, and the

Internet—so they are understandably skeptical about the authenticity of commercial messages. They seem to almost intuitively understand the manipulative nature of marketing, and as a group, they seem to develop disdain for any advertising that is obviously too slick, too neatly packaged, or too good to be true.

It has been estimated that the average person is barraged with more than 3,000 advertising messages per day, and some experts place the estimate much higher than 3,000. One would expect Baby Boomers, who only had to deal with a mere 560 messages daily in 1971, to experience some form of media overload in the twenty-first century. Yet somehow, their Millennial offspring seem to have become inured to the bombardment. Frustrated marketers have been pulling out their hair for more than 20 years, trying to figure out the magic solution for marketing successfully to Millennials.[2]

But since the early missteps of consumer giants Levi's and Nike, marketing professionals have indeed discovered many of the keys for successfully advertising to the younger generation. Many of the most successful have moved beyond traditional communication channels—print media, radio, and television—and developed successful campaigns utilizing the news media available to their target market: computers, the Internet, and mobile phones. And for good reason: A December 2008 report by marketing consultants Packaged Facts estimates that by the time most of the Millennials reach adulthood in 2017, their combined earnings will exceed $3 trillion annually![3] With that type of clout, clearly the members of the Millennial generation are a target demographic worth chasing.

The Marketing of a President

The U.S. presidential campaign of 2008 is a groundbreaking event that made history in many remarkable ways: the first viable female candidate for president, the first African American elected to the Oval Office, and the most comprehensive technology-based political campaign in U.S. history. No matter what side of the political spectrum one's sentiments dwell, it's very instructive to examine how Barack Obama's campaign team organized its marketing for the purpose of raising money and influencing voters' choices.

This is particularly true when you consider that Obama received more of the youth vote than McCain. By itself, this voting bloc did not put Obama into the White House. But coupled with the campaign's success with numerous other voter blocs, it certainly had a significant impact. In other words, the Obama campaign presents a nearly perfect blueprint for how to market successfully to the Millennial generation.

We need remember, however, that Obama was not the first to utilize digital strategies to market a candidate. In previous primaries, John McCain, Howard Dean, and President George W. Bush also relied rather heavily on online fundraising and digital marketing. But the 2008 Obama campaign raised digital marketing to extraordinary new heights.

Far beyond the level of other candidates, Obama's official web site smoothly steered visitors to join mailing lists, volunteer groups, fundraising lists, and local support groups at very nearly every turn of an Internet page. Not only was this well-designed web site easy to navigate, but the overall message was also inviting and inclusive: "Join us in making history." The overall experience for users was immersive—something that Millennials find particularly appealing.

And if for some reason you didn't find the primary Obama web site appealing or simply wished for a somewhat different experience, you also had the option of finding official Obama presences on a very wide variety of Web 2.0 destinations, such as Facebook, MySpace, Flickr, Twitter, Digg, LinkedIn, and nine other social-networking web sites. That may seem to be somewhat obtrusive, but keep in mind that it's really just a matter of customizing the experience to the customer's tastes: One person's Facebook may be another person's MySpace.

A unique feature of the Obama campaign's web presence was also the very high degree of coordination that was achieved by using the Internet to organize the time and efforts of thousands upon thousands of volunteers. In addition to receiving location assignments and shifts, the web site also encouraged people to form their own volunteer groups, and individual supporters were given the opportunity to create their own support page, allowing them to express opinions, post photos, list friends (à la Facebook), and communicate with fellow supporters.

The 2008 campaign was also marked by some purely creative uses of electronic media. For example, building on the immense popularity of Apple's iPhone, the Obama campaign made available for free an application that would allow iPhone users to check on their candidate's progress. Outside of the Obama web site, visitors to other locations on the Internet were also treated to a considerable amount of campaign advertising that cropped up on various search engines (notably Google).

Another particularly creative strategy was the placement of advertisements for candidate Obama within best-selling video games, such as *Madden 08*. These ads would cleverly appear as banner ads on billboards, scoreboards, or stadium walls within the games. It is not necessarily clear how many of the game players were of voting age, but the strategy also paid off because it generated a considerable amount of publicity in the media.

The campaign also employed the use of "viral marketing." Viral marketing is to the twenty-first century what word-of-mouth advertising was to the twentieth century. The viral-marketing strategy is to encourage people to voluntarily share marketing messages with their friends, particularly on the social-networking sites that we mentioned previously. In some cases, videos on YouTube or Flickr can garner millions of viewings. And while the Obama campaign officially uploaded numerous videos, there were also thousands of user-generated content (UGC) submissions, including homemade videos, animations, posters, mock commercials, and other media that made the rounds of Internet surfers.

Most people understand that running a political campaign is an expensive proposition. The importance of fund-raising in the 2008 campaign was no exception. Once again, history was made by the overall success of the Obama campaign in raising money. ABC News estimated that the final tally for President Barack Obama's fund-raising campaign was approximately $750 million, a truly breathtaking and unprecedented sum. The Obama campaign estimated that the total number of donors fell just below 4 million.[4] Only history will tell whether the success of the 2008 campaign will alter the face of future political campaigns, but it's a sure bet that future political campaigns will be technology driven.

Digital Consumers

All of the current generations have a history of technology. Baby Boomers first encountered technology in the 1960s, as corporations began to install mainframe computers and systematize their operations. Rumors were also present (and somewhat responsible for) the birth of the personal computer in the late 1970s. However, at a certain level, Baby Boomers' relationship with technology has always been a little tenuous. Certainly, there are many Boomers that have adopted a fairly technological lifestyle. But their experience can't be compared with the technology orientation of Generation X and the Millennials.

Generation X grew up experiencing a tremendous explosion of technical innovation during the 1980s. Not just personal computers, but also video games, cell phones, CD players, videotapes, and a host of other technologies were at their fingertips as they were coming of age. But the technological orientation of Millennials has been very different, even when compared with the experiences of Gen Xers.

The Millennial generation is the first generation that has truly been *immersed* in technology. Not only did they experience innovations that transformed the personal computer into a true information powerhouse, but they also grew up with what is possibly the greatest technological innovation in the twentieth century: the Internet. As is pretty readily acknowledged, the World Wide Web has become an almost infinite source of information and entertainment (sometimes even referred to as "infotainment"). And despite the Dot-Com Bust of 1999, the Internet has also been transformed into a tool that transcends productivity. Today, the Internet is almost as much a social tool as it is a technical and informational tool.

The late communication theorist Marshall McLuhan wrote in the early 1960s that television would have a tremendous impact on society by bringing people together into a type of "global village." His assertion that the "medium is the message" suggested that television would enjoy unprecedented influence and credibility because of the power of visual images to inform and persuade.[5] Many of his predictions proved prescient; however, in the early twenty-first century, they seem more applicable to the personal computer and the Internet.

For the members of Generation X, the Internet is a source of information. They communicate, explore, and learn online. Gen Xers enjoy researching and buying products and services over the Internet.

In contrast, Millennials use the Internet far more for social purposes than for commerce. Millennials seek out entertainment and look for opportunities to expand their social network online. The difference between the two generations is that Gen Xers use the Internet as a resource, while Millennials view it as an experience. Millennials don't merely want to take information away from the Internet: More than anything, they want to interact with the net. In some ways, you could say that the Millennial generation finds the Internet to be the greatest toy of all time.

A study by Deloitte LLP looked at differences in how the generations consumed various media. They found that the increasing merging of digital content with television is creating new patterns for consuming entertainment and information. They found:

- 51 percent of all consumers are watching and reading personal content created by others. The number jumps to 71 percent for Millennials.
- 55 percent of Millennials and 42 percent of Xers read blogs, while 62 percent of Millennials and 41 percent of Xers watch YouTube or other video-streaming sites.
- 40 percent of all consumers are creating their own entertainment, such as editing movies, music, and photos. Millennials may be the majority of the creators at 56 percent, but Matures are also participating—25 percent of them report creating their own entertainment.[6]

To be sure, the survey confirmed that Boomers and Gen Xers were also consuming Internet media, as well as radio and television media. But for Millennials, the creation of and consumption of UGC was a far greater slice of the media pie. Another survey, conducted by media-communication agency Universal McCann, also found a very clear trend toward the use of interactive, social media on the Internet. They found that among Millennials:

- 57.3 percent manage a profile on an existing social network.
- 52.2 percent upload photos to a photo-sharing web site.
- 67.5 percent read personal blogs or weblogs.
- 45.8 percent have left a comment on a news site.
- 82.9 percent watch video clips online.
- 45.1 percent have downloaded a podcast.[7]

Among the implications of the Millennial generation's penchant for engaging in social interactions over the Internet may well be some sweeping changes in how we manage the workforce. For example, although computer programs and web sites devoted to online collaboration between coworkers have existed for many years, it's likely that the Millennial generation will be the first to take genuine advantage of the possibilities. In addition, workplace communications are very likely to change, as Millennials begin to rely on chat and instant-messaging services in the office. It's also conceivable that more and more conferences that once required air travel and hotel stays will default to online events attended virtually by participants over the Internet. In many ways, we have to start looking at Millennials as a true real-time workforce that will tend to rely less on voice mail and e-mail, let alone snail mail, to get things done.

The Millennials may have a similar impact on e-commerce. Creating a truly immersive web experience today involves not only building an attractive web site that shows off your product or service to good advantage. It also has to involve visitors through engaging content. Interesting video clips, weblogs, contests, exclusive short videos, games, and instant messaging are all ways to create an immersive web experience, which is highly prized by Millennial consumers.

A model example of how marketers can use the Internet to engage consumers can be found at www.mentos.com, the official web site for Mentos mints. Mentos, which are produced by the Netherlands-based Perfetti Van Melle Corporation, have become very popular with Millennials, thanks in large part to a series of campy television commercials that began in the 1990s. In recent years, however, the company has tied its television campaigns in with clever web promotions that have generated a great deal of interest among young people.

Visitors to the site can view several videos of Mentos television commercials and order a personalized pocket bottle of Mentos gum (complete with the purchaser's name printed on the label, along with a personal custom picture and text message that the purchasers can upload). There is also a section where visitors can order official Mentos merchandise, such as caps and T-shirts, and another section where visitors can play a *Pac Man*–style Mentos game.

Another way marketers leverage the Web is by use of viral videos. These are just one example of what has come to be called "Web 2.0," a term that refers to a sort of second generation of web applications. While the underlying technologies of the Internet remain unchanged since the beginning, designers have sought ways to increase information sharing, collaboration, and functionality over the Internet. The results have been such phenomena as video-sharing sites, social-networking sites, blogs, wikis (collaborative information sites), and social-tagging sites (which provide quick links at the end of articles and presentations that allow visitors to make a rating of the content).

The lesson once again is that for the Millennial generation, the Internet is much more than simply a source of information or conventional entertainment. Millennials expect their time on the Internet to be immersive, interactive, and sociable. Those web sites that fall under the category of Web 2.0 provide precisely the types of experiences that keep Millennials engaged.

Hanging on the Telephone

Ironically, the tool that Millennials prefer for engaging in Internet-based interactivity may not be the personal computer, for which the Internet was originally created. Cell phones have become the constant companions of this generation. Phones provide not just voice contact with friends and family, but also a source for information gathering and relationship building. Millennials rely on their phones to serve as web clients, address books, calendars, cameras, shopping catalogs, music players, televisions, photo albums, and timepieces. And, oh yes—they also use them as telephones.

It was the Baby Boomers who first adopted cellular phones in large numbers. The appeal was irresistible: the ability to communicate with anyone, anywhere, no matter where *you* were. The value of cell phones for emergency purposes alone made a compelling reason to carry one in the car while driving. Of course, the early phones were cumbersome and somewhat confusing to use, while cell-phone coverage in the early years was spotty at best.

But as cell-phone technology improved dramatically, members of Generation X found them to be indispensable companions, whether on the job or at home. By the time the new Millennial generation began reaching teenage years, cell phones had become ubiquitous enough and affordable enough, so millions of parents gave cell phones to their offspring to use. And use them they did!

A September 2008 study by Knowledge Networks confirmed that Millennials are much more enthusiastic about using feature-rich phones on a daily basis.[8]

The study found:

- 61 percent of Millennial consumers say that on a cell phone, "the more features, the better," compared with 27 percent of Boomers.
- 32 percent say they call friends or family "all the time" or "often" when making shopping decisions, a figure that jumps to 45 percent among those whose ages are 18 to 34.
- Millennials send an average of 20 text messages daily, compared to just two for Generation X and less than one for Baby Boomers.

Obviously, there are ramifications for those marketing cellular technology. But there are also very clear ramifications for companies employing Millennials. Modern organizations can and must adapt their working style to fit the tools most widely used by the workers of their youngest generation. Restrictive policies on the use of cell phones, including text messaging, may put off a generation of workers who consider mobile phones to be their constant companions. It's not too far-fetched to say that somewhere down the road, mobile phones may actually replace the personal computer as the primary office tool.

The introduction of the iPhone by Apple Inc. heralded a revolution in the design and functionality of mobile phones. The iPhone joined the category called "smart phones," which provided users with functions well beyond placing and receiving telephone calls.

Although other products, such as the BlackBerry and the Palm Treo, also had various "office away from the office" features beyond calling, the iPhone was a game changer. It was the first phone to incorporate a revolutionary touch-screen system, making navigation and functionality seem like second nature. The iPhone also offered unprecedented integration with the user's personal computer so that both of those tools operated as a single system for the user.

A report by Rubicon Consulting in late 2008 showed that the most heavily used function of the iPhone was reading e-mail. The second-most popular function was mobile web browsing, which by consensus is a superior experience on the iPhone. While Apple's mobile device was expected to cut into an existing market among Windows Mobile phones and BlackBerrys, approximately 50 percent of iPhone users were replacing their conventional phones with iPhones. And for 10 percent of users, the iPhone was their first mobile device. The most telling finding showed that 20 percent of iPhone users said that they had discontinued carrying the personal computer in favor of their iPhone. And not surprisingly, about half of all iPhone users are below the age of 30.[9]

Needless to say, the success of Apple's mobile device has spawned a number of competitors offering similar touch-screen functionality, as well as integrating functions such as music players and on-demand video. Down the road, the use of videos on mobile phones may prove to have even more impact on how users interact with technology, as well as on how marketers connect with those users.

Try to imagine a single handheld device that can replace your home phone, personal computer, stereo system, satellite navigational system, DVD player, and television. The technology exists today already, and the implications for the future are difficult to imagine. But for those attempting to market to the Millennial generation, the actual media through which advertisers reach their target audience are evolving rapidly.

It may be too early to say that traditional channels for advertising and marketing are either dead or dying. Print media (including newspapers) and television seem to be entering challenging times. Where once they only had to compete with each other for advertising dollars, they now have to compete with the World Wide Web and new electronic media for the attention and the pocket-books of potential customers.

The new smart phones may eventually only be one part of the equation. But these feature-rich devices are successful precisely because they are the type of immersive technology demanded by the Millennial generation. And the generation has not shown a reluctance to fully exploit all of the features of the technology.

Word of Thumb

We live in a world that seems to be increasingly driven by personal opinions. This is readily apparent just by seeing how many television-news and current-events shows emphasize the sharing of opinions over the reporting of news. The line between the two seems to have become blurred, and even newscasters find themselves rendering opinions more frequently. Perhaps no medium, however, is more riddled with opinions, beliefs, judgments, predictions, and speculation than the Internet. Sometimes it can seem next to impossible to locate an objective opinion on the Internet, and yet a great many Internet users depend on the medium to research purchasing decisions.

The Millennial generation has a well-earned reputation for being skeptical of commercial messages and advertisers' blandishments. Having been bombarded with commercial messages since infancy, they've learned to take everything with a pretty large grain of salt. And yet, Millennials are easily influenced about matters of fashion and functionality by talking with their peers. The savviest marketers have come to realize that by creating a buzz among Millennials, they could create a demand for their products and establish a reputation for being a cool choice.

Since Millennials place so much credence in the opinions of their peers, it is inevitable that Web 2.0 applications develop mechanisms to allow site visitors to exchange their experiences, opinions, and product recommendations. Most mainstream retailing sites (sometimes called "e-tailers") incorporate some form of consumer-feedback rating system. Most mainstream retailers even provide feedback blogs where their customers can rate products and describe what they liked or disliked about the merchandise. Sites such as Amazon and Barnes & Noble provide customers with the opportunity to discuss their experiences. Several sites enable music lovers to share their opinions and recommendations, including iLike, iTunes, Last.fm, and MusicMatch. Movie lovers can weigh in on the Internet Movie Database (IMDB) or Netflix. Web sites such as Digg.com and StumbleUpon allow visitors to rate their favorite web sites.

The premise behind these collaborative web sites is really fundamental to human nature: People tend to solicit the opinions of people they like and trust. These web sites that have developed collaborative trust systems have widened the scope of what used to be called word-of-mouth advertising. Even though there is a type of mouth involved in collaborative-rating sites, we might better be served referring to them as "word-of-thumb" advertising. Marketers looking to extend their brand and increase sales have to pay attention to the groundswell of opinion that may exist on the Internet regarding their product or service.

Gaining Credibility with Millennials

In the late 1980s, the athletic shoe market was dominated by traditional brands, such as Nike, Adidas, Puma, Converse, and a few others. As mentioned previously, the mainstream marketers of athletic shoes missed the boat in their early marketing efforts directed at Millennials. However, southern California specialty-athletic shoemaker Vans began to hit the nail precisely on the head with their marketing in the 1990s. The marketers at Vans recognized that to reach their target audience—Millennial skateboarders, bicycle-motocross (BMX) racers, and snowboarders—they would have to position their advertising in the venues frequented by teenagers.

This led to Vans putting together a tour that featured extreme athletes showcasing skateboarding tricks combined with live bands performing hard rock music. The "Vans Warped Tour" became a kind of touchstone for marketers who wanted to capture the recognition, as well as the approval, of Millennials. It didn't take long for other marketers to also get on the bandwagon, sponsoring events targeted to teenagers. But skateboarding events and exhibitions were not the only way to reach the Millennial market.

The soft-drink market is dominated by the likes of Coca-Cola and Pepsi Cola, as well as Dr. Pepper. But in the mid-1990s, the Jones Soda Company of Seattle, Washington, positioned itself as the beverage for what it deemed to be the "alternative" market. Their strategy was to offer unusual flavors and to market their product directly to the Millennial generation in locations such as clothing stores, music stores, and tattoo parlors. Their goal was to gain a foothold with the younger generation, in which they succeeded admirably.

Millennials drank Jones Soda in increasing numbers and told their friends about it. Jones Soda, for its part, continued to produce innovative products, creative packaging, and immersive marketing techniques, such as selling cans of soda with custom labels designed and ordered by the consumer. Once again, word of mouth—if not actually word of thumb—prevailed over expensive marketing campaigns.

Even though Southwest Airlines has traditionally been the airline of business travelers, the company announced that they were sponsoring a midnight-gaming championship in 2008, targeted at gamers aged 16 to 25. Even though this demographic is very different than the business travelers Southwest typically courts, their marketing is looking long term toward a future in which the Millennial teenager of today will become the business traveler of tomorrow.

And even old dogs can learn new tricks. Procter & Gamble purchased the Herbal Essences beauty brand in 2001, but quickly realized that the brand had lost appeal for its core audience, middle-aged women. Rather than abandon the brand, Procter & Gamble decided to revitalize it, specifically targeting Millennial females. The effort included redesigning the line's packages to make it more youthful, renaming specific products, and placing the brand into stores that appealed more to younger women.

Increasingly, marketers are looking at ways to build relationships with Millennials. The traditional modes for reaching new target consumer groups—advertising in print, radio, and television—have given way as marketers have discovered that they have to reach the younger generation in new ways. Since the Internet provides a far higher degree of interactivity than any of the traditional media, it seems only logical that anyone seeking to connect with Millennials has to direct efforts in that direction. In order to be successful when marketing to them, you have to consider the following:

- **Millennials are media skeptics.** They have been bombarded with an inordinate amount of commercial messages every day since childhood, and they take everything they see and hear with a grain of salt. Avoid speaking down to or patronizing the Millennial generation when marketing your organization.
- **Sleek is cool.** The Millennial generation is particularly in love with products that are simple yet functional. They have a great sense of style when it comes to industrial design. The ideal model is Apple Inc., whose products particularly appeal to Millennials: the iMac, the iPhone, and the iPod, which have virtually become the prerequisite tools for an entire generation. Make sure new recruits to your organization are aware of state-of-the-art technology that you provide to employees, and consider contests and raffles of these sleek tools in your attraction and recruitment efforts.
- **You have to join the network.** Millennials, more than either of the preceding generations, are more comfortable in groups than in operating alone. This is true because they have been

raised to appreciate teamwork, partnership, and collaboration. They felt comfortable moving in large groups, and they have a very different, somewhat looser definition of what it means to be a friend. Showcase teamwork within your company to appeal to Millennials.

- **Meet them where they live.** As we've seen by now, the Millennials are experience driven. Marketers wishing to reach them with a message that resonates must take the message to them—to skate parks, concerts, clubs, shopping malls, and sporting events—in order to be heard. Use a variety of marketing venues and media to get the attention of Millennials (more ideas follow in this chapter).

- **Multichannel marketing rules.** An effective marketing campaign for the Millennial generation can't rely on just one advertising vehicle. Print and television ads have to be backed up with dynamic web sites. Viral videos must be involved, along with e-mail and instant messaging. Your web site needs to incorporate dynamic components from other media, such as YouTube. Utilizing a single channel by itself simply won't do in the twenty-first century. Make sure you use a variety of marketing channels to attract and recruit Millennials.

Those marketers who have managed to solve the puzzle of marketing to the Millennial generation have been rewarded with strong sales and powerful brand identity: Apple, In-N-Out Burger, Target, and Volkswagen, to name a few.

To be certain, brand loyalty is often fickle. And these brands may be no more than one marketing misstep or one negative headline away from losing their reputation with Millennials. But we are also dealing with a market that has huge potential—literally trillions of dollars in consumer spending over the next decade or so. Anyone seeking to attract Millennials to their product, service, or company needs to take proactive steps to reach this important audience.

Recruiting the Millennials

Another lesson can be learned when we consider the successes of those who are marketing to the Millennial generation. Corporate recruiters who recognize that they're going to have to attract, hire, and retain the most talented Millennials will also need to use approaches that are as creative and innovative as major marketers.

In the tight job markets that are going to occur over the next 10 years, organizations must create a reputation that would make them logical employers of choice for Millennials. As we mentioned earlier, that elusive quality of coolness that the Millennial generation attaches to famous brands can be hard to project. However, by making your presence known and directing some of your recruiting efforts to those places where Millennials live, you may be able to establish yourself as a cool organization. And you may even be able to put yourselves ahead of the competition.

Top Millennial candidates could be located in the following venues:

- **Student athletes**—The Millennial generation may actually have been one of the most athletically-oriented generations in history. In addition to official school-based teams, the Millennials participated in club teams, Little League, traveling teams, and various athletic association leagues. Your organization could consider sponsoring some of those teams, as well as becoming involved in team awards. Having visibility among the Millennials involved in local sports is a good way to raise your organization's identity. And don't forget about the potential leaders in athletics beyond the athletes themselves—the managers, trainers, coordinators, and mascots all demonstrate a high level of responsibility, commitment, and performance.
- **Business fraternities**—There are a number of Greek fraternities that are oriented toward helping their members to achieve success in business. Alpha Kappa Psi, Delta Sigma Pi, and Phi Chi Theta, among others, could prove to be good

sources for future job openings. Your organization may be able to sponsor charity events, advertise in fraternity publications, participate in charity fundraisers, or speak at their meetings.

- *Survivor* **and other reality show applicants**—It's very likely that local young people who have applied for, or even appeared in, network reality-TV shows may receive some publicity in local newspapers. This may give you a lead on potential applicants.

- **Internet cafés**—Visit a coffee shop or cyber café in any city or near any large college campus, and you most likely will find well-connected, Internet savvy, technically-oriented Millennials. They may even, from time to time, read business cards or flyers tacked to the cafés bulletin board—both nonelectronic and electronic ones!

- **Special-needs organizations**—Don't rule out recruiting from organizations that cater to special-needs groups. These individuals have had to work hard to achieve success, and they certainly have developed many of the skills your organization requires to be successful.

- **Gyms and work-out facilities**—The younger generation has grown up in a rather health-conscious environment (despite the rise in childhood obesity), and many members can be found exercising at health clubs and work-out facilities. Again, business cards and flyers can help you to establish a presence and may generate some interest among prospective employees.

- **Facebook, MySpace, LinkedIn, Twitter, and so forth**—As we've already established, the Millennial generation is very actively engaged in social networking on a very large scale. Your organization must have a presence on these sites, as well as a well-constructed and engaging web site.

- **Girl Scouts and Boy Scouts**—Among the most industrious future employees are members of two clubs: the Girl Scouts of America (especially those who receive the Gold Award) and the Boy Scouts of America (especially those who become

Eagle Scouts). Look for opportunities to sponsor Scout activities if possible, and consider supporting their organization's fund-raising activities.

- **Resident advisors in college dormitories**—We sometimes suspect that a necessary prerequisite for the job of United Nations ambassador should include time spent in college as a dormitory-resident advisor. Resident advisors need to be skilled communicators and proficient in resolving complex, often tough situations. They would no doubt make outstanding employees and leaders. (And yes—one of us was a resident advisor in college.)

- **High-school clubs**—Among the many after-school activities that Millennial high-school students can join are the 4H Club, the Rotary-sponsored Interact Club, and similar organizations. These clubs teach goal setting, planning, communication skills, and ethics. Students that have belonged to such organizations may well make ideal job prospects.

- **Entrepreneurial clubs**—Both in high school and college, there are many students who are geared toward a career as an entrepreneur. And while it may seem contradictory, students who are interested in entrepreneurship may also make very successful and effective corporate employees. Look for those who belong to the Distributive Education Clubs of America (DECA) and the Students in Free Enterprise (SIFE) clubs.

- **Military**—Armed forces are great technical and leadership builders. They can be a great source for future employees and leaders in your company.

As we previously pointed out, understanding what it takes to successfully market to Millennials is key to both establishing a positive organizational image and locating and recruiting the best talent that generation has to offer. Our insights into the mindsets of the younger generation can also be useful in helping to manage them more effectively. Either way, information is power, and we hope the information provides you with the power you need to recruit and employ this dynamic and energetic workforce.

Keys to Chapter 10

- Modern recruiting is as much about marketing as it is about talent management. Unless you can position your organization to young job candidates as an ideal place in which to develop a long career, you run the risk of losing millions of dollars in turnover and lost opportunities.
- Millennials grew up immersed in all sorts of media—print, radio, television, and the Internet—so they are understandably skeptical about the authenticity of commercial messages. They seem to almost intuitively understand the manipulative nature of marketing, and as a group, they seem to develop disdain for any advertising that is obviously too slick, too neatly packaged, or too good to be true.
- The average person is barraged with more advertising messages today than any previous generation.
- By sheer size, the Millennial generation stands to continue to increase its earning and spending power.
- For the members of Generation X, the Internet is a source of information. They research, explore, shop, and learn online.
- Millennials take to the Internet far more for social purposes than for commerce. Millennials seek out entertainment and look for opportunities to expand their social network online. The difference between the two generations is that Gen Xers use the Internet as a resource, while Millennials view it as an experience.
- The increased merging of digital content with television is creating new patterns for consuming entertainment and information, and more consumers and Millennials are watching and reading personal content created by others.
- Millennials clearly are using interactive and social media on the Internet. Many Millennials manage a profile on a social

network, upload photos to a photo-sharing web site, and read personal blogs and weblogs.

- Creating a truly immersive web experience today involves not only building an attractive web site that shows off your product or service to good advantage. It also has to involve visitors through engaging content. Interesting video clips, weblogs, contests, exclusive short videos, games, and instant messaging are all ways to create an immersive web experience, which is highly prized by Millennial consumers.

- Millennials rely on their phones to serve as web clients, address books, calendars, cameras, shopping catalogs, music players, televisions, photo albums, and timepieces.

- Millennials are much more enthusiastic about using feature-rich phones on a daily basis, as compared to previous generations.

- Restrictive policies on the use of cell phones, including text messaging, may put off a generation of workers who consider mobile phones to be their constant companions. It's not too far-fetched to say that somewhere down the road, mobile phones may actually replace the personal computer as the primary office tool.

11

Where to Start?

The beginning is the most important part of the work.

—Federico Fellini

For many organizations, the goal of attracting, hiring, and retaining Millennial employees may seem like a huge challenge. To be sure, it's not a process that should be taken lightly. While there may be a few lucky organizations whose identity is already well established among the younger generation, most firms will have to completely rethink their appeal to Millennials.

It's going to take more than a little window dressing or simple makeover to convince them that they should invest their future with you. It's going to take a complete rethinking of how your organization maximizes its human resources, starting from the top and extending all the way down to the smallest recesses of your company. Let's take a look at the strategies that can establish your firm as a truly cool place to work, one that creates organizational sustainability, growth, and profit.

Make a Commitment

As in most major change efforts, transforming an organization starts at the top. A senior executive team has to consider the value proposition—why it's going to pay off to attract and employ talented Millennials. This is important because there is a very real cost benefit to bringing Millennials on board. In terms of human capital, they represent not only the future security of your organization; they also offer the prospect of an immediate infusion of innovation and unprecedented energy levels.

Your senior leaders have to establish clear policies for attracting, selecting, developing, evaluating, and promoting Millennials, which in turn need to be communicated to all levels. There will need to be new ways of marketing the organization to prospects, and in many cases, the new marketing strategies will begin to also permeate strategies for marketing the organization's products or services. Don't forget, the Millennials will not only be your new talent pool—they're also your new customers!

Because you're going to be involving your executive team in making critical decisions about attracting and hiring Millennials, it only makes sense to directly involve them in the process. For example, if you establish a mentoring program, it would be wise to have some of your senior executives serving as participants. Obviously, changes in how your organization markets itself, whether to employment prospects or customers, will require the full support of senior management. And changes to your organization's overall image, a process that could meet considerable resistance among older executives, will have to be presented carefully in order to gain their cooperation.

You have to realize that it's not uncommon for an organization's most senior executives to be somewhat out of touch with the youngest employees, even though their children or grandchildren are of that generation. We've seen this many times in our consulting practice, but thankfully there are exceptions. More often than not, however, senior Baby Boom leaders expect young employees to earn their stripes before being allowed to advance up the ladder toward the executive suite.

A process of gradual integration and promotion of new employees like that would be fine in a world that was predictable and not subject to rapid change. But today we live in a global economy in which organizations have to be nimble and open to change in order to respond to the newest crisis or to seize an unexpected new opportunity. Flexibility and creativity are the order of the day!

In order to get your senior leaders on board with a concerted effort to attract Millennials, you have to help them make the connection between their organization's ability to turn on a dime and the presence of newer, younger employees. So, the first step toward becoming a truly cool organization may well start in the boardroom.

Creating a Cool Brand

Certainly, not every great company is a household name, but current business literature is populated with plenty of ubiquitous organizations such as Google, Starbucks, Whole Foods, Nordstrom's, Nike, and FedEx. In a nutshell, these are companies with plenty of curb appeal.

But what do *those* employers have that other organizations lack? Well, clearly these employers are engaged in cool pursuits and offer lots of perks and benefits. But there is also something about the way they manage their employees that makes them cool.

And yes, we recognize that these are very large corporations with lots of resources and very powerful marketing capabilities that are tough to compete with, but compete with them you must! Your organization probably has a lot to offer new employees, but you have to be able and willing to communicate why your organization is the best place for a young employee to make a start. It may not just be fat salaries and copious benefits that make the difference when you're trying to attract talented young employees.

Take Google, for example. If most organizations had to match what Google has to offer materially, there would be no contest. Google would win! But look more closely. Besides good pay, benefits, and creative perks like car-washing and hair-styling services, Google also offers a very dynamic work environment. Employees are encouraged to innovate and are given time to pursue new ideas. Google is also very creative in how it assigns work and defines job titles.

And don't forget to take a look at your organization's vision, mission, and values as potential cool factors in attracting Millennials. They like to feel that the work they do contributes something to the greater good of society. If you can show them that type of contribution as a result of their efforts, your organization should definitely be on their short list of cool companies.

Even if you cannot duplicate the pay and benefits plan of a Google, your organization can still replicate some aspects of its work environment. But bear in mind that it will take actions first, not just words, to project your company as a truly cool place in which to work. Fortunately, you can accomplish this by examining your organization's workplace environment and by working with the HR department to make it more dynamic.

Partnering with Human Resources

Creating a flexible, dynamic, and energizing work environment doesn't require massive amounts of capital. It does, however, require a certain amount of risk taking and a fresh way of looking at your organizational environment. Most importantly, as we stated previously, it requires the commitment of the senior team. A Millennial-friendly environment is a multigenerational-friendly environment. If time is not spent to create such an environment, friction among the generations and the certain exodus of Millennials will continue to cause massive dollar losses. The senior team's most critical internal partner is the human-resources team, since HR should be the best skilled in talent-attraction and retention strategies.

The senior team–HR partnership should consider workplace policies that can provide employees with a lot of flexibility while maintaining a productive structure. It's about more than adding a few personal days a year. It's about concepts like job sharing, work teams, flextime, virtual work, and flexible benefits.

Putting it all together—the type of work that your organization performs, combined with the way that jobs are designed, the type of atmosphere within which employees collaborate, and the way the organization goes about developing and promoting employees—should make it easy to present a very compelling portrait of what makes your company cool.

Then when you have a handle on your organization's cool rating, you can begin to brand yourself in ways that will garner the attention of your Millennial job candidates. Additionally, work with internal and external public relations and communication professionals to make sure that any and all communication job candidates are likely to see and hear—the organizational web site, promotional literature, television commercials, and so forth—are designed or redesigned to reflect those cool factors. Keep your organization's representatives, such as recruiters, well versed in the talking points that explain why your organization is a cool place to work.

By the same token, anyone charged with the responsibility of interviewing a Millennial job candidate should also be well trained to respond to questions about the cool elements in the workplace and to sell such features to the young candidate. This type of job interview may be a little different than the traditional approach that many employers are accustomed to.

The overall goal is not just to weed out undesirable candidates. Part of the goal is to sell the organization to the most talented candidates in order to bring aboard a dynamic new group of employees. You need to make sure that all of your interviewers—especially non-HR representatives—grasp this dual purpose. It's just as likely that recruits will decide which company to join based on personal interactions and a gut feeling about the organization's work environment and about how stimulating the job will be.

But to be able to convey the type of working environment your organization offers, you have to understand something about its culture.

Taking an Organizational Pulse

One of the best ways that we know to gain a solid perspective on your company's work culture or personality is to take an organizational pulse—in other words, an organizational survey.

To do this effectively, you are going to have to rely on the cooperation of both management and employees, but you may even want to consider feedback from customers and vendors.

It is important to determine the type of information you want. From there, you can work with an external provider to customize a survey for you. It is critical that you commit to taking action on what the survey reveals before you administer it. For example, if you know that you can't increase salaries, why ask employees about their level of satisfaction with their compensation? Assistance from an expert external provider should ensure that the survey items are worded behaviorally and normed for validity and reliability.

There are several methods that lend themselves to this type of survey. Web-based assessments with multiple-choice answers—usually utilizing a five-point scale from "strongly agree" to "strongly disagree"—are the best way to gain the broadest possible range of responses.

What follows are sample survey items taken from a wide variety of KEYGroup's customized organizational surveys:

- The organization's policies have been effectively communicated to me.
- Good communication exists between my manager and me.
- The organization offers me options for career advancement.
- The organization tries to retain qualified employees.
- My job environment is a safe place to work.
- Good communication exists between our location and headquarters.
- I have been adequately trained to perform my present job.

- I am given training opportunities to prepare me for the future with this organization.
- If I were offered a similar job at similar pay with a different employer, I would choose to stay with this organization.
- I can make certain decisions on my own, without having to ask my manager first.
- I have a good working relationship with my manager(s).
- I know that doing my job the right way is important to the company.
- The organization I work for is committed to providing superior products and services to its customers.
- Overall morale at my location is positive.
- The organization holds employees accountable for their performance.
- The organization is committed to quality and continuous improvement.
- I am able to participate in decisions that affect my area.
- I believe that my organization treats its employees with integrity.
- The organization respects the importance of my personal life.
- I would recommend working at my organization to my friends.
- I think that the organization is headed in the right direction.
- I think that the organization provides excellent service to our clients and customers.
- I enjoy the work I do for my organization.
- I have the tools and resources necessary to do my job.
- My job makes good use of my skills and abilities.
- I can take initiative and try new things to improve the way we do things.
- I get the information I need to do my job.
- I know my job affects the success of the company.
- My manager clearly communicates what he or she expects of me.

- My manager encourages me to continually improve my work.
- I can speak frankly to my manager about things that concern me.
- I can speak openly and honestly to anyone in the company, including senior management.
- I am offered challenging work.
- My manager's expectations of me are realistic.
- My manager gives me help when I need it.
- My performance reviews let me know how I can improve my performance.
- I am fairly compensated for the work that I perform.
- The organization has adequately communicated policies and procedures to me.
- The company's benefits program meets my needs.
- I'm confident that senior management will make the right decisions for the organization to be successful.
- The senior management team is approachable.
- The organization keeps me well informed about the company's business objectives.
- The organization keeps me well informed about the company's plans for the future.
- My productivity on the job suffers because the company causes unnecessary stress.
- My company has given me clearly defined goals for my job.
- I get feedback on my performance at least one time per week.
- I plan to look for another job this year so that I can have a life.

In addition to using survey items similar to the examples provided, be sure to provide opportunities for open-ended suggestions and comments.

Assessments like these give you a read on your organization and a chance to look at your organization through the eyes of a prospective employee. Depending upon the results, you can determine where your organization has strengths and identify where further development may be needed when it comes to employee attraction and retention.

You may add to your survey information by conducting focus groups, or you may conduct focus groups alone. When bringing together employees for these face-to-face discussions, remember to limit the size to 8 to 10 employees, to use a trained facilitator, and to ensure a cross-section of employees. Another option for focus groups is to group employees by generation in order to identify and resolve potential conflict situations. Before actually administering the survey and conducting the focus groups, make sure to protect employee anonymity and make a commitment to respondents to provide a summary of the results and actions to be taken.

Another valuable tool in addition to organizational assessment is the use of individual assessments. We use what we believe to be the best assessments on the market, Profiles International. Assessments can be used for selection, development, team building, executive coaching, and succession planning.

And don't forget about keeper interviews that we discussed earlier. There's no better way to learn the shortcomings and strong points of an organization than to ask employees in order to prevent them from moving on. If conducted properly, as indicated previously in Chapter 6, you will be able to solicit honest feedback about what should be done differently. So, if you can handle the unvarnished truth, the information that keeper interviews yield should be pretty valuable.

And don't forget about feedback from employees gathered in performance-management discussions and exit interviews. Once again, these could provide you with valuable ammunition to help you improve your organization's workplace culture.

Reviewing Human Resources Processes

While you're in the process of making your organization attractive to all job candidates, this is also a good time to conduct an overall audit of your human-resources processes. Too often we find that in many organizations, the human-resources department has become bogged down in the routine of dealing with reporting and oversight functions, such as legal compliance and risk management. It can be all too easy for the HR department to lose sight of the corporate mission.

The role of HR is not to merely enforce legalities, rules, and procedures. Human resources should also be focused on making sure that the organization has a workforce with the talent and skills necessary to respond to both present and future challenges. With regards to recruitment and selection, it's vital for the HR department to understand the organization's present needs and future potential. Maintaining close relationships with line managers is critical for HR to understand the types of skills and education you need to be looking for in new employees.

It is also important for HR to maintain a working relationship with some of the other staff departments, such as finance and information technology, to develop some perspective on the potential future needs as the organization continues to grow. Human resources professionals also need to maintain a regular dialog with senior executives that may have some very strong opinions about the future of the organization.

Sometimes, we suspect that a successful HR professional should be a cross between a professor of employment law and a fortune teller with a crystal ball! It's obviously difficult to predict what the future holds for any organization, but there can be little doubt that the solution to *your* future problems will come from your Millennial employees as they move up the organization. Finding the right ones to begin with is obviously critical.

However, they won't move up the organization unless you have performance discussions that are designed to provide valuable, constructive feedback. It's time for antiquated, stodgy performance-management systems to be thrown out. Current performance-management systems need to be dynamic, with a strong emphasis on frequent coaching and regular feedback. Consider instituting a performance-coaching system that encourages employees to self-assess their progress while gathering input, feedback, and guidance from their managers, peers, mentors, and even customers.

Also, if you expect Millennials to invest in a long career within your organization, they need to have sessions that allow them to explore a clear path of advancement. So, career-development policies and procedures are also an important aspect of HR management to review.

Do your career-development strategies reflect the realities of your organization? Do they provide clear and balanced opportunities based on achievement? Do they make provisions for effective learning and development to ensure your future executives have the necessary skills? Finally, is there a policy for promotion that is fair and equitable and that will put the right person into the right position at the right time?

This ultimately leads us to the question of succession planning. We've found in our consulting that this is often one of the weakest areas in human resources management. Perhaps it's because human beings don't typically like to contemplate their own endpoint. Perhaps it's because looking that far into the future may seem like an exercise in futility. But the record shows that those organizations with solid long-term succession-planning policies are the most stable and the best positioned for future growth.

With each new incoming cohort of Millennials, you need to ask yourself, "Which of these has the most potential to someday succeed the top leaders of our organization?" By beginning early to groom your top Millennial prospects for the future, you'll be able to provide the right training and employment experiences that will someday result in very well-qualified, highly competent, experienced, and visionary leaders for your organization.

Keys to Chapter 11

- For many organizations, the goal of attracting, hiring, and retaining Millennial employees is going to take a complete rethinking of how the organization maximizes its human resources.

- Senior leaders have to establish clear policies for attracting, selecting, developing, evaluating, and promoting Millennials, which in turn need to be communicated to all levels.

- There will need to be new ways of marketing the organization to prospects, and in many cases, the new marketing strategies will begin to also permeate strategies for marketing the organization's products or services.

- In order to get your senior leaders on board with a concerted effort to attract Millennials, you have to help them make the connection between their organization's ability to turn on a dime and the presence of newer, younger employees.

- Look at your organization's vision, mission, and values as potential cool factors in attracting Millennials. They like to feel that the work they do contributes something to the greater good of society.

- A Millennial-friendly environment is a multigenerational-friendly environment. If time is not spent to create such an environment, friction among the generations and the certain exodus of Millennials will continue to cause massive dollar losses.

- The senior team–HR partnership should consider workplace policies that can provide employees with a lot of flexibility while maintaining a productive structure.

- Anyone charged with the responsibility of interviewing a Millennial job candidate should also be well trained to respond to questions about the cool elements in the workplace and to sell such features to the young candidate. This type of job interview may be a little different than the traditional approach that many employers are accustomed to.

- One of the best ways to gain a solid perspective on your company's work culture or personality is to take an organizational pulse—in other words, an organizational survey. To do this effectively, you are going to have to rely upon the cooperation of both management and employees, but you may even want to consider feedback from customers and vendors.

- The role of HR is not to merely enforce legalities, rules, and procedures. Human resources should also be focused on making sure that the organization has a workforce with the talent and skills necessary to respond to both present and future challenges.

- Professionally-developed assessments provide leaders with the data to make informed decisions in a fact-based and validated manner, giving them the metrics to track cost-savings and return on investment. This method takes very little time, is very inexpensive, and is highly objective rather than subjective. Assessments are time-tested, indispensable tools for leaders. We use Profiles International assessments to target all phases of employment from hiring to development and succession-planning.

Notes

Chapter 1: A Generational Battle Ahead

1. Betty W. Su, "The U.S. Economy to 2016: Slower Growth as Boomers Are Set to Retire," *Monthly Labor Review* 130, no. 11 (2007): 13–32.

2. Mitra Toossi, "Labor Force Demographic Data: Medium-term Projections to 2016," U.S. Department of Labor, Bureau of Labor Statistics, June 18, 2008. Available at http://www.bls.gov/emp/emplab1.htm.

3. "OPEN Ages Survey," OPEN from American Express, April 26, 2007. Available at http://home3.americanexpress.com/corp/pc/2007/geny.asp.

4. Mark McCrindle, "New Generations at Work: Retaining Gen Y," Community Active Careers: Work that Matters! October 10, 2007.

5. Morris Massey, *The People Puzzle: Understanding Yourself & Others* (Reston, VA: Reston Publishing, 1979).

6. Dr. Richard Mullendore, Professor, University of Georgia.

7. Robert Half International and Yahoo!HotJobs, "What Millennial Workers Want: How to Attract and Retain Gen Y

Employees," 2007. Available at http://www.hotjobsre-sources.com/pdfs/MillennialWorkers.pdf.

8. John Naisbitt, *Megatrends: Ten New Directions Transforming Our Lives* (New York: Warner Books, 1982).

9. The Henry J. Kaiser Family Foundation, "Media Multi-tasking: Changing the Amount and Nature of Young People's Media Use," news release, March 9, 2005. Available at http://www.kff.org/entmedia/entmedia030905nr.cfm.

Chapter 2: A Workforce to Reckon With

1. The survey was entitled "Monitoring Your Future" and was conducted by Jean Twenge and W. Keith Campbell in 2008.

2. Masaya Takahashi and Heihachiro Arito, "Maintenance of Alertness and Performance by a Brief Nap after Lunch under Prior Sleep Deficit," *Sleep* 23, no. 6 (2000): 813–19.

3. Motorola Home and Networks Mobility, "Motorola Survey Reveals Media Mobility is Key for the Millennial Generation," news release, September 10, 2008. Available at http://mediacenter.motorola.com/Content/Detail.aspx?ReleaseID=5831&NewsAreaID=2

Chapter 3: Attracting Millennials . . . The "Cool Factor"

1. *BizTimes Milwaukee* (formerly *Small Business News*), "What Makes Future 50 Companies Cool?" September 14, 2007. Available at http://www.biztimes.com/news/2007/9/14/what-makes-future-50-companies-cool.

2. Forrester Consulting (prepared for Xerox), "Is Europe Ready for the Millennials? Innovate to Meet the Needs of the Emerging Generation," November 2006. Available at http://www.ffpress.net/Kunden/XER/Downloads/XER87000/XER87000.pdf.

Chapter 4: Those *Other* Children of Boomers . . . Generation X

1. U.S. Census Bureau, Facts for Features, "Mother's Day: May, 2008," press release, March 13, 2008. Available at http://www.census.gov/Press-Release/www/releases/archives/cb08ff-08.pdf.

2. BBC News, "More Women Have a Late Pregnancy," December 17, 2004. Available at http://news.bbc.co.uk/1/hi/health/4104033.stm.

3. Jeff Gordinier. *X Saves The World: How Generations X Got The Shaft But Can Still Keep Everything From Sucking* (New York: Penguin Group, 2008).

4. Tammy Erickson, "Ten Reasons Gen Xers Are Unhappy at Work," *Businessweek,* May 10, 2008. Available at http://www.businessweek.com/managing/content/may2008/ca20080515_250308.htm.

5. Jane Deverson and Charles Hamblett, *Generation X* (London: Tandem Books, 1964).

6. Douglas Coupland, *Generation X: Tales for an Accelerated Culture* (New York: St. Martin's Press, 1991).

7. David M. Gross and Sophfronia Scott, "Proceeding With Caution," *TIME,* July 16, 1990.

8. T. Paul Schultz, ed., *Research in Population Economics,* vol. 6 (Greenwich, CT: JAI Press, 1988).

Chapter 7: Millennial or Boomer?

1. Morris Massey, *The People Puzzle: Understanding Yourself & Others* (Reston, VA: Reston Publishing, 1979).

2. Eric Greenberg and Karl Weber. *Generation We: How Millennial Youth are Taking Over America and Changing Our World Forever* (Emeryville, CA: Pachatusan, 2008).

3. Abby Kiesa and others, "Millennials Talk Politics: A Study of College Student Political Engagement," Center

for Information and Research on Civic Learning and Engagement (CIRCLE), 2008. Available at http://www.civicyouth.org/PopUps/CSTP.pdf.

4. Eric Greenberg and Karl Weber (2008).

Chapter 8: Preparing Millennials to Lead

1. Josephson Institute of Ethics, "2008 Report Card on the Ethics of American Youth," 2008. Available at http://charactercounts.org/programs/reportcard/.

2. Alan Lakein. *How to Get Control of Your Time and Your Life* (New York: Penguin Group, 1974).

3. Thomas Friedman. *The World is Flat: A Brief History of the Twenty-first Century* (New York: Picador, 2005).

Chapter 9: R U Communicating with Millennials?

1. Douglas Coupland, *Generation X: Tales for an Accelerated Culture* (New York: St. Martin's Press, 1991).

2. J.D. Lasica, "The Mobile Generation: Global Transformations at the Cellular Level," Aspen Institute, 2007. Available at http://www.aspeninstitute.org/atf/cf/%7BDEB6F227-659B-4EC8-8F84-8DF23CA704F5%7D/C&S_The_Mobile_Generation.pdf.

3. A.T. Kearney and Judge Business School, "Study Finds Mobile Phone Users Embracing Mobile Data Services," news release, November 3, 2005. Available at http://www.atkearney.com/main.taf?p=1,5,1,167.

Chapter 10: Marketing to Millennials

1. Ellen Neuborne, "Generation Y," *Businessweek,* February 15, 1999. Available at http://www.businessweek.com/archives/1999/b3616001.arc.htm#B3616001.

2. David Shenk. *Data Smog: Surviving the Information Glut* (New York: HarperCollins, 1997).

3. Packaged Facts, "The Adults of Generation Y in the U.S.: Hitting the Demographics, Lifestyle and Marketing Mark," December 1, 2008.

4. Tahman Bradley, "Final Fundraising Figure: Obama's $750M," ABC News, December 5, 2008. Available at http://abcnews. go.com/Politics/Vote2008/story?id=6397572&page=1.

5. Marshall McLuhan and Lewis H. Lapham, *Understanding Media: The Extensions of Man* (Cambridge, MA: MIT Press, 1994).

6. Deloitte LLP, "Are You Ready for the Future of Media? Highlights from Deloitte's 2007 'State of the Media Democracy' Survey," 2007. Available at http://www.deloitte. com/dtt/article/0,1002,cid=156096,00.html.

7. Universal McCann, "Power to the People: Social Media Tracker Wave 3," March 2008. Available at http://www .universalmccann.com/Assets/wave_3_20080403093750.pdf.

8. Knowledge Networks/SRI, "How People Use Cell Phones," 2008.

9. Rubicon Consulting, "The Apple iPhone: Successes and Challenges for the Mobile Industry," March 31, 2008. Available at http://rubiconconsulting.com/downloads/whitepapers/ Rubicon-iPhone_User_Survey.pdf.

About the Authors

Joanne G. Sujansky, PhD, CSP (Certified Speaking Professional)

Joanne G. Sujansky, PhD, CSP, CEO of KEYGroup, has worked with leaders to make their workplaces more productive and to help them retain top talent. Her expertise, insight, wisdom, humor, and practical solutions have made Joanne a highly sought-after speaker for keynote addresses. Her consulting and speaking talent has been tapped by executives in thirty-five countries.

Joanne has authored numerous articles and books on leadership, change, and retention. She wrote *The Power of Partnering: Vision Commitment and Action*, published by Pfeiffer; coauthored *Training Games for Managing Change*, published by McGraw-Hill; and seven additional books, published by KEYGroup.

Joanne, who founded KEYGroup in 1980, is an award-winning entrepreneur. Earlier in her career, she held management- and director-level positions across several different industries. She is past national president of the American Society for Training and Development (ASTD) and is a recipient of their highest honor, the Gordon M. Bliss Award. An active member of the National Speakers Association (NSA), she has received their highest-earned designation, Certified Speaking Professional (CSP).

For more information, please visit www.joannesujansky.com.

Jan Ferri-Reed, PhD

Jan Ferri-Reed, PhD, is a seasoned consultant and President of KEYGroup, a 29-year-old international speaking, training, and assessment firm. Jan has presented a variety of programs to thousands of managers and employees in a diverse range of organizations across the globe. Jan's work focuses on creating productive workplaces and retaining talent. She does executive consultation; facilitation of senior level, planning, and team-building retreats; and keynoting at corporate and association events.

Representative clients for whom Jan provides services include GlaxoSmithKline, MARC Advertising, DelMonte Foods, the Bank of New York Mellon Corporation, US Steel Corporation, Volkswagen-Audi-Porsche, Pitney Bowes, MTV Networks, Merrill Lynch, and UBS-AG. Additionally, she served as an adjunct professor to the Human Resources Management program at LaRoche College. Jan and the KEYGroup team use Profiles International assessments to augment their consulting and training projects.

Jan is an active member of the American Society for Training and Development (ASTD), the HR Leadership Forum, and the Pittsburgh Human Resources Association (PHRA). She has also served on the Board of the Association for The Arc and on the Advisory Board of the Association for Children and Adults with Learning Disabilities. Her doctoral work was completed at the University of Pittsburgh, where her studies focused in the areas of consultant ethics and organization development.

For more information, visit www.keygroupconsulting.com.

Index